SIMON&SCHUSTER
HANDBOOK
FOR WRITERS

CAROLYN CHRISTENSEN WEST

Daytona Beach Community College

STUDY GUIDE
TO ACCOMPANY
SIMON&SCHUSTER
HANDBOOK
FOR WRITERS

LYNN QUITMAN TROYKA

PRENTICE-HALL, INC., Englewood Cliffs, N.J. 07632

Printed in the United States of America.

10 9 8 7 6 5 4 3 2 1

ISBN 0-13-810491-3 01

Prentice-Hall International (UK) Limited, London
Prentice-Hall of Australia Pyt. Limited, Sydney
Prentice-Hall Canada Inc., Toronto
Prentice-Hall Hispanoamericana, S.A., Mexico
Prentice-Hall of India Private Limited, New Delhi
Prentice-Hall of Japan, Inc., Tokyo
Prentice-Hall of Southeast Asia Pte. Ltd., Singapore
Editora Prentice-Hall do Brasil, Ltd., Rio de Janeiro

CONTENTS

PREFACE

This Study Guide is designed to accompany The Simon & Schuster Handbook for Writers by Lynn Quitman Troyka. The guide can be used as a preview before reading each chapter in the Handbook, and as a review after reading each chapter. The Guide can also be used as an aid in preparing for chapter quizzes and tests. Each chapter in the Guide corresponds to a chapter in the Handbook, and each Guide question is keyed to direct you to a particular section of the Handbook for further explanation and review. For example, the notation (4b) indicates that the particular question focuses on material concerning paragraph development in Chapter 4, section "b" of the Handbook.

Each chapter in the Study Guide has been divided into three sections:

1. KEY TERMS AND CONCEPTS: In this section important terms are listed in the order of their appearance in the Handbook. Preview these terms before reading the chapter. Then, as you read, note definitions and examples of these various terms. You may want to write them on flash cards for review. Some terms will reoccur in several chapters of the Handbook, so take advantage of the chance to gather new examples and reinforce your learning.

2. FILL-IN QUESTIONS: These questions review main points in each chapter. Try covering the answers on the right hand side of the page and filling in the blanks. As you proceed, check your answers against the correct ones. If any of your answers are incorrect or you have doubts about your own response, go back to the section in the Handbook indicated in the parentheses in order to review the concept.

3. MULTIPLE-CHOICE QUESTIONS: These questions are intended to test your ability to apply the writing suggestions, rules and concepts you have been studying in the Handbook. For each item, mark the answer you believe is correct. Then compare your answers with the correct one listed at the end of the test. If you have

missed any, turn to the section of the Handbook indicated in the parentheses at the right of each question. Review the section and then reexamine the entire question. Look at the alternative answers; remember that knowning why choices are incorrect is as important as knowing the correct answer. (In a few chapters, the multiple-choice questions have been omitted)

By reading the text chapters carefully and by using the Study Guide as I have suggested, you should be better prepared for quizzes and tests as well as better able to write clearly and effectively.

I wish to especially thank the following people for their help in preparing this Study Guide: Ms. Myrtle Almire, for her patient typing and corrections; Dr. Donnetta Heitschmidt, for her helpful scheduling and support; and my mother, Ms. Martha Christensen, for her invaluable proofreading and babysitting.

Carolyn Christensen West
Daytona Beach, Florida

SIMON&SCHUSTER
HANDBOOK
FOR WRITERS

1

THINKING ABOUT PURPOSES AND AUDIENCES

KEY TERMS AND CONCEPTS

communication
message
thesis
narration
description
exposition
argumentation

purpose for writing
audience
general reading public
tone
instructor as reader
specialist as reader

FILL-IN QUESTIONS

1. Writing is a way of _____ a message to   communicating
   a reader for a purpose. (1a)

2. The _____ of a piece of writing refers   purpose
   to what the writer seeks to achieve, what the aim
   or intention is. (1b)

3. In _____ writing, the two most common   academic
   purposes are to inform the reader and to persuade
   the reader. (1b)

4. Informative or _____ writing focuses   expository
   on the subject being discussed and includes
   reports of observations, ideas, scientific data,
   facts, statistics, etc. (1b)

5. Persuasive or _____ writing focuses on   argumentative
   its readers and seeks to convince them of a position
   that is a matter of opinion. (1b)

6. Effective persuasive writing, which includes that found in editorials, reviews, sermons, business or research proposals etc., does not merely state an opinion but offers convincing _____ for it.   (1b)

support

7. Good writing is often judged by the success it has in communicating its message to its intended _____.   (1c)

audience

8. Writers need to know who their readers will be and what amount of education and experience they have as well as as what general and specialized _____ _____ they have about the subject.   (1c)

knowledge

9. Additionally, writers may lose their audience if they are not _____ to their reader's beliefs concerns and preconceptions.   (1c)

sensitive

10. Although the general reading public is educated, it expects the material to be clear and free of advanced _____ information; it also expects to be treated respectfully.   (1c)

technical

11. Student writers cannot assume that their instructors and others in the general reading public will mentally _____ what is missing on the page; thus, they must be careful not to leave out material.   (1c)

fill in

12. _____ are members of the general reading public who share knowledge, assumptions, interests and beliefs about the subject. The reader with this audience must balance the need to be thorough with the need to avoid redundancy. (1c)

Specialists

2
PLANNING AND SHAPING

KEY TERMS AND CONCEPTS

writing process
essay
paper
topic
purpose
audience
special requirements
invention techniques
idea book
journal
freewriting
focused freewriting
brain storming

journalist's questions
mapping (webbing)
shaping (composing)
levels of generalizing
climactic (emphatic) order
chronological order
spatial order
tone
thesis statement
informal outline
formal outline

FILL-IN QUESTIONS

1. When you are cast into a writing situation, in the process of gathering and thinking through ideas for your topic, you need to establish a _____, or point of view, toward your topic, as well as support for it.   (2b)

   focus

2. Special _____ include the time alloted for your assignment, its length, and other practical constraints, all of which must be considered when you make decisions about your topic, purpose and audience. (2b)

   requirements

3. What separates most good writing from bad is the writer's ability to move back and forth between _____ statements and specific details. (2c)　　　　　　general

4. Some _____ techniques to gather ideas for writing include keeping an idea book or a journal, freewriting, brainstorming, using journalist's questions, and knowing when to read other sources for information. (2d)　　　　　　invention

5. Keeping a daily _____ gives you the habit of producing writing, instills the habit of close observation and thinking, as well as serving as an excellent source of writing ideas. (2d)　　　　　　journal

6. Sometimes focused on a set topic, _____ is writing nonstop, writing whatever comes to mind, letting your mind make all sorts of associations in the search for interesting ideas to write about. (2d)　　　　　　freewriting

7. Making a quick list of all the ideas that are associated with a topic, a technique called _____, also lets your mind range freely, generating quantities of ideas at random which may then be grouped as relationships become apparent. (2d)　　　　　　brainstorming

8. Asking the journalist's questions, Who?, What?, When?, _____?, Where? and How?, can expand ideas for writing by forcing you to approach a topic from several different perspectives. (2d)　　　　　　Why

9. During the shaping or composing process, you will make connections, find patterns and put the related ideas you have gathered into group determining which ideas are more _____ and which are more specific. (2e)　　　　　　general

10. When shaping ideas, you may use one of these three common patterns: climactic order, which moves from least to most important; _____ order, which presents ideas according to a time sequence; and _____ order, which presents ideas arranged according to their physical locations in relation to one another. (2e)　　　　　　chronological

　　　　　　spatial

11. As an adult writing to an adult audience, you are expected to maintain a reasonable and moderate _____ (which should sound midway between the informal and the highly formal) appropriate to your specific topic, audience and purpose. (2e)　　　　　　tone

4

12. The _____ statement contains the essay's main idea, the central point you are making to your readers. (2e)

thesis

13. The thesis also reflects the essay's main _____ (either to inform or to persuade) and its focus (your point of view) and may briefly state the major subdivisions of the essay. (2e)

purpose

14. A preliminary thesis statement is often too _____ or too vague and, therefore, must be narrowed and more clearly focused through successive drafts of the essay. (2e)

broad

15. An _____ outline, which does not have to follow all the formal conventions of outlining, is a working plan, a layout of the main points and subordinate ideas and details that can be useful in planning the final order of the paper. (2e)

informal

3
DRAFTING
AND
REVISING

KEY TERMS AND CONCEPTS

drafting
revising
composing
first draft
discovery draft
thesis statement
unity
coherence

distancing
revision checklist
editing
editing checklist
proofreading
word processor

FILL-IN QUESTIONS

1. "Drafting" may be a more accurate word than "writing" because it conveys the idea that the final product of the writing _____ is the result of a number of versions, each successively closer to what the writer intends and what communicates most clearly to the reader. (3)   process

2. Even experienced, successful writers get blocked, but they try to suspend _____ and get something on paper to work with, knowing that good writing takes time and patience, knowing that a first draft is not meant to be perfect but to be revised. (3a)   judgment

3. The _____ statement expresses the central idea that controls and limits what the essay will cover. (3b)   thesis

4. The thesis statement contains the topic narrowed appropriately for the writing situation, a focus that

presents what you are saying about the topic, and a
_____ which is either informative or
persuasive. (3b)

purpose

5. The direction of drafting is _____, so
writers must keep pressing ahead and not be so worried
about possible stylist problems and grammatical/
mechanical errors that they get sidetracked from the
task of pulling together sentences and paragraphs
into a unified whole. (3b)

forward

6. An essay has _____ when the thesis statement
clearly ties into all topic sentences, and the support
for each sentence (paragraph development) contains
examples, reasons, facts and details directly related
to the thesis statement. (3b)

unity

7. An essay is _____ when it has signals (such
as transitional expressions, pronoun repetition and
parallel structures) that communicate the relationship among the ideas in the essays. (3b)

coherent

8. Although the idea gathering stage needs a suspension
of hasty critical judgment to allow the mind free
access to a range of possibilities, the _____
stage of the writing process requires evaluation in
order to decide where improvements are needed. (3c)

revision

9. Two major activities during revision are adding by
inserting needed words, sentences or paragraph, and
_____ by getting rid of whatever goes off
the subject or repeats unnecessarily what has already
been said. (3c)

cutting

10. Revision also involves replacing material as needed
by substituting new words, sentences and paragraphs
for what has been cut, as well as _____
material around by changing the sequence of sentences
and paragraphs for clearer logical connections. (3c)

moving

11. A revision _____ can help you focus your
attention in an organized and efficient way as you
revise your essay; one type of checklist, which moves
from the whole essay to paragraph to sentences to
words, works well for many writers. (3c)

checklist

12. When _____ is constructive, you can learn a
great deal about your writing through the eyes of
others since they often take a more _____
view of your material. (3c)

criticism

objective

13. In contrast to revising, editing focuses more on
_____ than on meaning. (3d)

presenta-
tion

14. When you _____, you check your final version   proofread
    carefully to see that it is an accurate and clean tran-
    scription of your final draft.   (3e)

6.

graph developed
separate subject
must have some u
mon.   (4d)

14. Paragraphs using

_____
developed either
which moves back
aspects of the t
using the _____
one subject comp
(4d)

15. An introductory
ductory _____
anecdote, questi
reader interest

_____
devices as it su
action, or point

4
WRITING
PARAGRAPHS

MULTIPLE-CHOICE QUEST

Selection I--

Like many city
black walnuts the ha
in New Jersey, I was
pods that I picked a
stained hands were g
Lenape Indians knew,
hair instead of my h
trying to open them,
rate, I learned why
found on supermarket

1. The topic senter
    A) occurs as th
    B) is implied
    C) follows a de
    D) is found on

2. Selection I has
    A) reasons and
    B) names, examp
    C) numbers and
    D) numbers, exa

KEY TERMS AND CONCEPTS

paragraph
topical paragraph
topic (main idea sentence
limiting (clarifying) sentence
unity
deductive reasoning
inductive reasoning
support (development)
RENNS
coherence
transitional expressions
pronoun "bridges"
selective repetition
parallel structure
from general to specific
from specific to general
from least to most important
from problem to solution
spatial sequence
chronological sequence

narration
description
process
example
extended definition
analysis (division)
classification
comparison
contrast
point-by-point structure
block structure
analogy
cause-and-effect analysis
introductory paragraph
introductory devices
concluding paragraph
concluding devices
transitional paragraph

FILL-IN QUESTIONS

1. A paragraph has _____ when all its sen-   unity
    tences relate to the main idea.   (4a)

2. The _____ sentence, which contains the   topic
    main idea of a paragraph, focuses and controls what
    can appear within the paragraph.   (4a)

3. Paragraphs whe[...]
   lowed by suppo[...]
   pattern called[...]
   moves from the[...]

4. Paragraphs tha[...]
   moving from sp[...]
   build suspense[...]
   the main point[...]

5. Paragraphs can[...]
   RENNS, an acro[...]
   names, numbers[...]
   (4a)

6. When the sente[...]
   each other, no[...]
   grammatical st[...]
   paragraph is s[...]

7. Words and phra[...]
   ideas, called [...]
   help achieve c[...]

8. Pronoun "bridg[...]

   _____
   parallel struct[...]
   help make writ[...]

9. A method of ar[...]
   according to l[...]
   sequence, desc[...]
   relative to on[...]
   of reference.

10. When a narrativ[...]
    logical sequenc[...]
    happening durin[...]
    (4c)

11. Descriptive wri[...]

    _____
    taste--while a [...]
    describes a seq[...]
    is done or made[...]

12. A paragraph dev[...]
    pattern uses il[...]
    idea, but a par[...]
    _____ devel[...]
    the meaning of [...]

13. A paragraph dev[...]
    one subject int[...]

outside, always dancing, always flicking out his lightning left jab. It isn't one punch, but the accumulation of punches that wears his opponents down. Leonard sets up his opponents with combinations of punches and when they drop their guard, he strikes like a cobra. He throws so many punches and so fast that you can only count them on slow motion replay.

10. The pattern of development for Selection IV is (4d)
    A) classification.
    B) climactic.
    C) comparison.
    D) contrast.

11. The structure used for dealing with the two subject in (4d)
    Selection V is
    A) point-by-point.
    B) block.
    C) parallels.
    D) cause-and-effect.

ANSWERS TO MULTIPLE-CHOICE QUESTIONS

1 - A	4 - C	7 - B	10 - D
2 - B	5 - D	8 - B	11 - B
3 - C	6 - C	9 - A	

14

5
THINKING CRITICALLY

KEY TERMS AND CONCEPTS

analysis
synthesis
evaluation
critical thinking
SQ3R
inferences
author's tone
prejudice
unstated assumptions
evidence
primary evidence
secondary evidence
premises
induction
deduction
validity
oversimplification

fallacy
hasty generalization
analogy
false analogy
circular argument
"non-sequitur"
"post hoc, ergo propter hoc"
self-contradiction
red herring
"ad hominum"
bandwagon
"ad verecundiam"
special pleading
dilemma
false dilemma
ambiguity
equivocal

FILL-IN QUESTIONS

1. Einstein's asking Hoffman to "Please go slowly" emphasizes that critical thinking, involving processes of contemplation and deliberation, requires _____. (5)   time

2. Critical thinking is rooted in analysis (taking ideas apart), synthesis (making connections among ideas) and _____ (determining the   evaluation quality of the ideas. (5)

3. One key activity in the dynamic, meaning-making process of reading is making _____ or guessing what is coming next. (5a) — predictions

4. The SQ3R method of critical reading involves _____ (or skimming) and questioning; next comes the actual reading and then _____ (or recalling) and reviewing as ways of reinforcing the meaning of the passage. (5a) — surveying / reciting

5. The three levels of the reading process are the literal or "reading on the line," the _____ _____ (or "reading between the lines") and finally the evaluative (or "reading beyond the lines"). (5b) — inferential

6. Becoming aware of alternate interpretations, of irony, and of the author's background, philosophy and biases requires making _____ during the reading process. (5b) — inferences

7. A major evaluative reading skill is differentiating between fact and _____. (5b) — opinion

8. Even though cast in subjective language, a statement may still be factual, depending on the intent and authority of its _____. (5b) — author

9. First-hand evidence provided by direct _____ _____ is called primary evidence, while secondary evidence is provided by the opinions of experts on the subject. (5c) — observation

10. People should not trust an assertion or conclusion if it is based on only some members of a group being discussed because the evidence may not be a _____ sample of the group. (5c) — representative

11. Conclusions are more reasonable if they are _____ with words such as "some," "many," "may," "possibly" etc. (5c) — qualified

12. The strength or value of the reported observation hinges on the _____ of the observer. (5c) — reliability

13. Current material, written in relatively objective language by an expert on the subject, appearing in a reputable publication, can usually be considered a _____ source. (5c) — reliable

14. Looking for clear relationships (more than merely chronological) without oversimplification and with a pattern of _____ can help when you evaluating cause-and-effect relationships. (5d) — repetition

15. _____ is the process of arriving at   **Induction**
general principles from particular facts or in-
stances. (5e)

MULTIPLE-CHOICE QUESTIONS

Selection I

    Elvar and Tolva were separated from one another. Each dolphin was
confined in a small, narrow space at the end of a common tank. Each could
hear the other's voice through the water but they could not see each other.
Each had its own hydrophone and its sounds were recorded on separate tapes.
Under these conditions, the animals emitted whistles which were usually
politely alternating, first one and then the other, with monologues and
some short duets (with beats, yet!).

John C. Lilly M.D.--<u>Man and Dolphin</u>

Selection II

    Another Monaco insider agreed that Caroline and Braghieri are involved
in a romance. "They scarcely bother to disguise their feelings for each
other in front of Stefano. I myself have seen them kiss each other."

1. Both Selection I and II involve reported observation, but   (5c)
the information reported in Selection I is more reliable
that that reported in Selection II because
  A) Selection II does not name the "insider" so no real
      authority can be established.
  B) Dr. Lilly is a well-known and respected biologist.
  C) Dr. Lilly's information is more specific and detailed.
  D) all of the above.

2. In Selection II, the insider apparently concludes that two   (5d)
people are involved in a romance because they kiss each
other. The insider
  A) may be oversimplifying.
  B) is demonstrating self-contradiction.
  C) establishes a false analogy.
  D) all of the above.

3. In Selection I, we can infer from the author's use of the   (5d)
terms "politely," "monologue," and "duet" that he has con-
cluded that the dolphins
  A) are as intelligent as human beings.
  B) were communicating with each other.
  C) were suffering in captivity.
  D) both (A) and (B)

Selection III

The sign says "You are entering the Green River Soil Conservation District." In smaller type is a list of who is cooperating; the letters are too small to be read from a moving bus. It must be a roster of who's who in conservation. The sign is neatly painted. It stands in a creek bottom pasture so short you could play golf on it. The new creek bed is ditched straight as a ruler; it has been "uncurled" by the county engineer to hurry the run-off. On the hill in the background are contoured strip-crops; they have "curled" by the erosions engineer to retard run-off. The water must be confused by so much advice.

Aldo Leopold--A Sand County Almanac

4. In Selection III the author seems to be (5b)
   A) unbiased, merely objectively describing the landscape.
   B) in favor of the conservation efforts he describes.
   C) opposed to the engineering of nature.
   D) both (A) and (C)

5. In Selection III the third sentence ("It must be a roster of (5b) who's who . . . .") shows that the author
   A) means literally a list of well known people.
   B) suggests an exaggerated self-importance of these people.
   C) knows everybody on the list.
   D) both (A) and (B)

Selection IV

"Four Seasons [greenhouses] did the complete
remodeling job and their product is terrific!
That's why Four Seasons is our favorite
remodeling contractor."

Mr. and Mrs. Joseph Galiano
Bellport, NY

6. The greenhouse ad in Selection IV features a photo of a (5b) smiling couple in a glass enclosure. The product advertiser expects readers to conclude
   A) that Four Seasons greenhouses are terrific.
   B) that Mr. and Mrs. Galiano are pleased with Four Seasons.
   C) that Mr. and Mrs. Galiano are the smiling couple in the photo.
   D) probably all of the above.

7. Readers need to avoid concluding that Four Seasons green- (5f) houses are "terrific" on the basis of the ad because it may be
   A) card-stacking or using special pleading.
   B) a red herring or ignoring the question.

C) using "ad hominum" or an appeal to the person.
D) probably all of the above.

8. The Archbishop of Canterbury recently urged his bishops to   (5f)
   reject a motion that would allow women ordained by the
   Anglican Church abroad to conduct services in England on
   the grounds that it would "threaten the unity of the church."
   His argument rests on the premise that women do not make
   satisfactory priests. His argument is an example of
   A) unstated assumption.
   B) hasty generalization (stereotyping).
   C) bandwagon.
   D) both (A) and (B)

9. An ad for a handheld tiller: "Because the Mantis is a   (5f)
   tough, durable precision instrument, the tines are so strong
   they're guaranteed for life." The ad is guilty of
   A) appeal to ignorance.
   B) false or irrelevant authority.
   C) circular argument.
   D) both (A) and (C)

10. Dr. Lilly argued: "If they [dolphins] can learn even a very   (5e)
    primitive version of one of our languages . . . this would
    raise them to the proto-humanoid, if not the humanoid, level--
    that is, it will prove that they have an intellectual capacity."
    His argument is thus:

               Language ability is proof of intellectual capacity.
               Dolphins have language capacity.
                        Therefore,
               Dolphins have intellectual capacity.

    Lilly's argument reaches a
    A) valid conclusion by deduction.
    B) invalid conclusion by deduction.
    C) reliable conclusion by induction.
    D) unreliable conclusion by induction.

ANSWERS TO MULTIPLE-CHOICE QUESTIONS

1 - D	4 - C	7 - A	10 - A
2 - A	5 - D	8 - D	
3 - B	6 - D	9 - C	

6
PARTS
OF
SPEECH

KEY TERMS AND CONCEPTS

function (within a sentence)
part of speech
proper noun
common noun
concrete noun
abstract noun
collective noun
mass noun
plural
article
antecedent
personal pronoun
relative pronoun
interrogative pronoun
demonstrative pronoun
reflexive pronoun
intensive pronoun
reciprocal pronoun
indefinite pronoun
main verb

linking verb
auxiliary verb
verb
infinitive
past participle
present participle
gerund
descriptive adjective
limiting adjective
proper adjective
conjunctive adverb
prepositional phrase
coordinating conjunction
correlative conjunction
subordinating conjunction
interjection
expletive

FILL-IN QUESTIONS

1. Understanding the parts of speech helps us identify
    how a word_____ in the specific sentence   functions
    in which it appears (6)

2. Names of specific people, places or things (where
    the first letter is always capitalized) are called
    _____ nouns. (6a)   proper

3. Nouns that name things that can be seen, heard,
    smelled or tasted are called_____   concrete
    nouns. (6a)

20

4. When a noun such as "mouse" changes its form to "mice," it does so to indicate a change from _____ to plural form. (6a)

singular

5. Sometimes called "noun markers" or "noun determiners," the little words "a," "an" and "the" are more commonly referred to as _____. (6a)

articles

6. The word (or words) a pronoun refers to or replaces is called its_____. (6b)

antecedent

7. A linking verb is a main verb that connects the subject of a sentence with a subject_____ --a word or words that describe or rename the subject. (6c)

complement

8. Auxiliary or_____ verbs are forms of the verbs "to be," "to do," "to have" etc. that combine with the main verb to create verb phrases. (6c)

helping

9. _____ are verb parts such as "wanted" or "swimming" that function as nouns, adjectives or adverbs in a sentence. (6d)

verbals

10. Some words quite different from descriptive adjectives still function as they do to limit _____ _____, so they too are classified as adjectives. (6e)

nouns

11. Indefinite, interrogative, numerical, possessive and relative adjectives can also function as _____ _____, so we must see them in the context of a sentence in order to identify their part of speech. (6e)

pronouns

12. An_____ can modify (describe or limit) verbs, adjectives, adverbs and even entire sentences. (6f)

adverb

13. A prepositional phrase always has a preposition connected to a noun or pronoun_____. (6g)

object

14. _____ conjunctions join two or more grammatically equivalent structures. (6h)

coordinating

15. Subordinating conjunctions begin certain _____ clauses, joining them to an independent clause to create a complex sentence. (6h)

dependent

MULTIPLE-CHOICE QUESTIONS

1. Words that name "uncountable" things such as coffee or sand   (6a)
    are classified as
    A) collective nouns.
    B) mass nouns.
    C) plurals.
    D) indefinites.

2. A noun such as "fear" would best be classified as   (6a)
    A) proper.
    B) common.
    C) concrete.
    D) abstract.

3. In the sentence "Kim took the watch that my grandfather had   (6b)
    given me," the pronoun "that"
    A) introduces an adjective clause modifying "watch."
    B) reflects back to the antecedent "Kim."
    C) refers to nonspecific things.
    D) both (A) and (C)

4. In the sentence "Kim confessed that he had stolen it himself,"   (6b)
    the last pronoun is
    A) personal.
    B) demonstrative.
    C) reflexive
    D) reciprocal.

5. In the sentence, "They loved each other very much," the terms   (6b)
    "each other"
    A) intensify the antecedent.
    B) refer to individual parts of a plural antecedent.
    C) are reciprocal.
    D) both (B) and (C).

6. In the sentence "Rosa looked flushed with excitement," the   (6c)
    term "flushed"
    A) describes the subject.
    B) is a complement.
    C) expresses action of the subject.
    D) both (A) and (B).

7. In the sentence "Her new boyfriend was coming to Rosa's   (6c)
    party," the words "was coming" are
    A) a complement.
    B) a verb phrase.
    C) a verbal.
    D) both (B) and (C).

8. "A baked potato, without the sour cream and butter, has about   (6d)
    the same number of calories as an apple." In the preceding
    sentence, the term "baked" is
    A) an infinitive.
    B) a past participle.

22

C) a present participle.
D) a gerund.

9. "To succeed is the secret wish of almost everyone." In the above sentence, the "to succeed" can be classified as   (6d)
   A) an infinitive.
   B) a past participle.
   C) a present participle.
   D) a gerund.

10. "Running has become a popular way of strengthening the heart." In the above sentence, the term "running" is   (6d)
   A) an infinitive.
   B) a past participle.
   C) a present participle.
   D) a gerund

11. In the sentence "These keys will open the lock," the terms "these" and "that" are   (6e)
   A) demonstrative pronouns.
   B) demonstrative adjectives.
   C) indefinite adjectives.
   D) none of the above.

12. "They wondered whose clothes were lying on the river bank." In the preceding sentence, the adjective "whose" would best be classified as   (6e)
   A) interrogative.
   B) numerical.
   C) possessive.
   D) relative.

13. "The couple could not communicate; finally, they got counseling help to resolve their differences." In the preceding sentence, the word "finally"   (6f)
   A) creates a logical connection between clauses.
   B) is a conjunctive adverb.
   C) shows relationship of time.
   D) all of the above.

14. "Many advertisements on commercial television use emotional appeals instead of hard evidence about product advantages over other competitors." The above sentence   (6g)
   A) is a single independent clause.
   B) contains noun objects in prepositional phrases.
   C) contains only two prepositional phrases.
   D) both (A) and (B).

15. "Some doctors believe it is the attitude of patients that ultimately decides whether they live or die." In the above sentence, the word group "whether they live or die" is a construction that   (6h)

A) uses subordinating conjunctions.
B) joins grammatical equivalents.
C) joins two independent clauses.
D) both (A) and (B).

ANSWERS TO MULTIPLE-CHOICE QUESTIONS

1 - B	5 - D	9 - A	13 - D
2 - D	6 - D	10 - D	14 - D
3 - A	7 - B	11 - B	15 - B
4 - C	8 - B	12 - C	

7
BASIC PARTS
AND STRUCTURES
OF THE SENTENCE

KEY TERMS AND CONCEPTS

simple subject
complete subject
compound subject
simple predicate
complete predicate
compound predicate
direct object
indirect object
subject complement
object complement
appositive
phrase
noun phrase
verb phrase
prepositional phrase
absolute phrase
verbal phrase

infinitive phrase
gerund phrase
participial phrase
clause
independent (main) clause
dependent (subordinate) clause
adverb clause
subordinating conjunction
adjective (relative) clause
relative pronouns
noun clause
elliptical clause
simple sentence
compound sentence
complex sentence
compound-complex sentence

FILL-IN QUESTIONS

1. A _____ subject is the (or group of words)   simple
   that acts, is described, or is acted upon; the _____   complete
   _____ subject includes the word (or groups of words)
   as well as its (their) modifiers--words that describe or
   limit it (them). (7a)

2. A subject can be _____; that is, it can consist   compound
   of two or more nouns or pronouns and their modifiers.
   (7a)

3. The _____ contains the verb and tells what the subject is doing or experiencing or what is being done to the subject. (7a)

    predicate

4. A _____ object receives the action or completes the meaning of a transitive verb. (7b)

    direct

5. An _____ object answers the questions "To whom?" and "For whom?" about the verb. (7b)

    indirect

6. A subject _____ is a noun or adjective that follows a _____ verb (such as "are" or "was") signaling that the subject is being renamed or described in the predicate of the sentence. (7c)

    complement
    linking

7. Adverbs can modify (or describe) _____, adjectives and other adverbs as well as _____ _____ clauses. (7c)

    verbs
    independent

8. An _____ is a word (or words) that renames a noun or words functioning as a noun; commas should be inserted between it and what it renames. (7c)

    appositive

9. A _____ is a group of related words that does not contain a subject or a predicate; therefore, it cannot stand alone as an independent unit. (7d)

    phrase

10. A verbal phrase is a group of words that contains a verbal (an infinitive, a gerund, a _____ participle or a _____ participle). (7d)

    past
    present

11. Clauses (word groups that contain a subject and a _____) are classified as either independent (also called _____) clauses or dependent (also called _____) clauses. (7e)

    predicate
    main
    subordinate

12. A dependent clause, containing its subject and predicate, usually starts with a _____ conjunction (such as "after" or "because"), a word that implies that the clause meaning is dependent on and must be attached to an _____ clause. (7e)

    subordinating

    independent

13. _____ clauses usually answer some questions (such as "How?", "Why?", "When?" or "Under what conditions?") about independent clause, thus modifying the entire clause. (7e)

    Adverb

14. Another type of dependent clause, the relative or _____ usually begins with a relative pronoun (such as "who", "that" or "which") and

    adjective

refers to a specific antecedent in the independent
clause it is attached to and modifies. (7e)

15. When a simple sentence (a single independent clause)
is attached to one or more dependent clauses, they
combine to create a _____ sentence. (7e)   complex

MULTIPLE-CHOICE QUESTIONS

1. "The stranded family was being helped by Navy helicopters   (7a)
lowering rescue lines." In the above sentence
   A) the simple subject acts.
   B) the compound subject is described.
   C) the simple subject is acted upon.
   D) both (A) and (C)

2. "Several great white sharks were spotted near their foun-   (7a)
dered boat." In the above sentence, the words "several
great white"
   A) describe or limit the simple subject.
   B) modify the noun "shark."
   C) receive the action of a transitive verb.
   D) both (A) and (B)

3. "The seventeen year old son had tried the radio and managed   (7a)
to get help on the way." This sentence has
   A) a complete subject.
   B) a compound subject.
   C) a compound predicate.
   D) both (A) and (C)

4. "No one saw the shark attack because of the chop created by   (7b)
the whirling propellers." In the above sentence, the words
"shark attack"
   A) are part of the predicate.
   B) function as a direct object.
   C) indicate that they are an indirect object.
   D) both (A) and (B)

5. "The medic immediately gave the youngest boy, age twelve,   (7b)
two pints of blood." In this sentence, the words "youngest
boy"
   A) act as a direct object.
   B) function as an indirect object.
   C) are an object complement.
   D) all of the above

6. "The boy was alive when they got him to the hospital" Here   (7c)
the term "alive"
   A) follows a linking verb.
   B) renames or describes the subject.
   C) is a subject complement.
   D) all of the above

7. "However, the boy seemed very badly injured." The preced-   (7c)
   ing sentence contains
   A)   a subject complement.
   B)   an object complement.
   C)   an adverb modifying an independent clause.
   D)   both (A) and (C)

8. "The boy's doctor, an expert surgeon, was able to save his   (7c)
   right leg." In the above sentence, the expression "an ex-
   pert surgeon"
   A)   is the subject of the sentence.
   B)   is an appositive.
   C)   is a part of the predicate.
   D)   both (B) and (C)

9. "He remained in critical condition for several days." The   (7d)
   above sentence contains
   A)   two noun phrases.
   B)   a verb phrase.
   C)   two prepositional phrases.
   D)   an absolute phrase.

10. "Several marine biologists speculated that the sharks never   (7d)
    would have attacked if the water had not been so disturbed."
    In additional to a noun phrase, the above sentence contains
    A)   two verb phrases
    B)   a prepositional phrase that modifies the subject.
    C)   an absolute phrase.
    D)   all of the above.

11. "Sensing panic and frenzy, the sharks must have rushed to   (7d)
    feed in the choppy water." The above sentence begins with
    A)   a noun phrase.
    B)   a participial phrase using a present participle.
    C)   a participial phrase using a past participle.
    D)   a gerund phrase.

12. "The sharks may never have seen the boy at all because their   (7e)
    vision is very poor." The above sentence
    A)   contains a subordinating conjunction.
    B)   is a complex sentence.
    C)   contains an adverb clause.
    D)   all of the above.

13. "However, sharks have a well developed lateral line which is   (7e)
    extremely sensitive to vibrations in the water." The above
    sentence
    A)   contains a relative pronoun.
    B)   contains an adjective clause.
    C)   is a compound sentence.
    D)   both (A) and (B)

14. "Fear must have become fascination, and the boy later became   (7e)
    a biologist who specialized in shark study." The above sen-
    tence

28

A) contains an adjective clause.
B) contains an adverb clause.
C) contains a coordination conjunction joining two main clauses.
D) both (A) and (C)

15. "Although they have a sinister appearance, sharks are the   (7e)
    most gracefully streamlined of all fish." The above sen-
    tence
    A) contains an adverb clause.
    B) contains an adjective clause in the independent clause.
    C) uses a noun clause to modify the subject.
    D) both (A) and (C)

16. "Since sharks are heavier than water, they avoid sinking by   (7f)
    sweeping their asymmetric tail, which provides the necessary
    lift, and they use their flat pectoral fins as planes." The
    above sentence
    A) is a simple sentence.
    B) is a compound sentence.
    C) is a complex sentence.
    D) is a compound-complex sentence.

ANSWERS TO MULTIPLE-CHOICE QUESTIONS

1 - C	5 - B	9 - C	13 - D
2 - D	6 - D	10 - A	14 - D
3 - D	7 - D	11 - B	15 - A
4 - D	8 - B	12 - D	16 - D

8
VERBS

KEY TERMS AND CONCEPTS

verb
person
number
tense
mood
voice
main verb
auxiliary (helping) verb
past tense
past participle
present participle
regular verb
irregular verb
linking verb
transitive verb
intransitive verb
modal auxiliary verb

simple present tense
past perfect tense
present perfect tense
future perfect tense
past progressive tense
present progressive tense
present perfect progressive tense
future perfect progressive tense
independent clause
dependent clause
indicative mood
imperative mood
subjunctive mood
active voice
passive voice

FILL-IN QUESTIONS

1. A verb reports on an action ("She hit the ball."), an occurrence ("The accident happened there.") or a state of _____ ("The day seemed hot.") (8)   being

2. Verbs usually change form by adding an _____;   ending
   these changes help deliver information about tense, indicating whether an action occurred in the past, present
   or _____. (8)   future

3. The _____ (or base) form of a verb shows action taking now, in the present (except for the third person singular). (8a)

    simple

4. The past tense and past _____ form of many irregular verbs either change their spelling or make use of different words instead of adding an _____ ending as regular verbs do. (8a)

    participle

    -ed or -d

5. Verbs also have a _____ participle form, created by adding "-ing"; like the past participle, it needs an _____ (or helping) verb in order for it to function as a verb instead of a modifier. (8a)

    present

    auxiliary

6. Present tense verbs in the simple form must show agreement with third person singular noun and pronoun subjects by adding an _____ ending. (8a)

    -s or -es

7. Speakers who tend to skip over the "-s" or "-es" endings on present tense verbs following third person singular subjects as well as "-ed" or "-d" endings on past tense and past participles tend to forget to add it in their _____ English and therefore, must _____ carefully. (8a)

    written
    proofread

8. The most common and most irregular verb in English, _____ functions along with "do" and "have" as either an _____ or a main verb; as a main verb, it _____ or joins a subject to a subject complement which renames or describes the subject. (8c)

    "be"
    auxiliary
    links

9. _____ auxiliary verbs (such as "could", "may", "should", "must" and "ought to") have only one form and add a sense of need, possibility, obligation, permission, or ability. (8c)

    Modal

10. A _____ verb must attach to a direct object, which receives the action of the verb ("He set the table."); an _____ verb does not require an object or receiver of the action to complete the meaning of the sentence ("They usually sit here."). (8d)

    transitive

    intransitive

11. The simple _____ tense describes what is happening, what is true at the moment or what is consistently true; the _____ tense tells of a completed action or a condition now ended while the _____ tense indicates an action to be taken or a condition not yet experienced. (8e)

    present

    past

    future

12. The _____ perfect tense generally indicates that an action (or its effect) in the past continues into the present; the _____ perfect tense describes a condition or action that started in the past, continued for a time and then ended; the _____ perfect tense indicates an action that will have been completed or a condition that will have ended by a specific time in the future. (8e)

present

past

future

13. All six of the above tenses also have _____ forms which show an ongoing or continuing dimension to whatever the verb describes; these forms are created by adding an _____ or helping verb to the "-ing" form or the present participle. (8g)

progressive

auxiliary

14. The tense of the verb in an independent clause of a complex sentence determines what verb tenses must be used in its _____ clause; accurate tense sequence is necessary to show the correct _____ relationship within the sentence. (8h)

dependent
time

15. The focus is on the subject's performing an action in a sentence written in the _____ voice, while the focus shifts to the object's receiving an action in a sentence written in the _____ voice. (8j)

active

passive

MULTIPLE-CHOICE QUESTIONS

1. "During the trial, the judge was so sure that the defendant (8a) had changed his testimony that she ordered a lie detector test." In the above sentence the verbs
   A) report an action.
   B) repot an occurrence.
   C) report a state of being.
   D) all of the above.

2. In the sentence that begins question #1, the term "ordered" (8a) is used as
   A) a past participle.
   B) a present participle.
   C) a main verb in the past tense.
   D) all of the above.

3. "The jury was deliberating for several hours." The verb (8a) phrase in this sentence
   A) contains a present participle.
   B) is in a progressive form.
   C) contains a gerund.
   D) both (A) and (B)

4. "Of course everyone wants fair trials as well as just and humane decisions." The verb in this sentence (8a)
   A) follows a third person singular subject.
   B) is in plural form.
   C) is possessive.
   D) both (A) and (B)

5. The correct past tense of the verb "cry is (8b)
   A) similar to that of "obey".
   B) cryed.
   C) cried.
   D) both (A) and (B)

6. "They had thought that the teacher was prejudice because he was suppose to give the test when he had promised he would." In the above sentence, there is (8b)
   A) an error in the first and second participle.
   B) an error in the second and third participle.
   C) an error in the third and fourth participle.
   D) no error in verb phrases.

7. Which of the following verbs is an incorrect past tense form? (8b)
   A) stole
   B) hanged
   C) frozen
   D) rang

8. Which simple form verb does not change its spelling when it is used in the past tense? (8b)
   A) bite
   B) fight
   C) eat
   D) cut

9. Which past tense form does not change its spelling when the verb is used as a past participle? (8b)
   A) swam
   B) swung
   C) threw
   D) rose

10. The past participle form of "be" is (8c)
    A) been
    B) was
    C) were
    D) being

11. "The couple watched the eleven o'clock news." In the preceding sentence the term "watched" (8d)
    A) is followed by a direct object.
    B) is a linking verb.
    C) is a transitive verb.
    D) both (A) and (C)

33

12. "My father should stop smoking because he has emphysema."   (8c)
    The modal auxiliary in the above sentence conveys
    A)   the past tense meaning of the verb.
    B)   a sense of obligation.
    C)   both possibility and permission.
    D)   both (A) and (B)

13. "Because it helped him breathe, he lay sleeping in the chair   (8d)
    until dawn." In the above sentence the verb "lay"
    A)   is past tense intransitive.
    B)   should be spelled "laid" instead.
    C)   is past tense transitive.
    D)   is present tense transitive.

14. "Mother quit smoking after she had read about the effects of   (8f)
    'second hand' smoke." In the above sentence the verb phrase
    "had read"
    A)   is in the past perfect tense.
    B)   in in the past progressive tense.
    C)   indicates that an action was completed before another
         action took place.
    D)   both (A) and (C)

15. "In the later stages, the disease will have been weakening   (8g)
    the blood's ability to transmit oxygen and can thus affect
    the brain." The verb phrase "will have been weakening"
    A)   shows that an action will continue for some time.
    B)   is in the future perfect tense.
    C)   uses a progressive form of the future tense.
    D)   both (A) and (C)

16. "Because of new warnings, the number of smokers has been   (8g)
    declining in recent years." The verb phrase in the above
    sentence
    A)   shows a future action that will continue.
    B)   describes something going on in the past that is likely to
         continue in the future.
    C)   indicates something taking place at the time it is written
         or spoken.
    D)   both (B) and (C)

17. "The public has become aware of the hazards of smoking since   (8h)
    the Surgeon General . . . ." To complete the complex sen-
    tence above, the dependent clause
    A)   requires a past tense verb.
    B)   requires a present perfect tense verb.
    C)   requires a past perfect tense verb.
    D)   either (B) or (C)

18. "Dad wishes he were not addicted to cigarettes." The pre-   (8i)
    ceding sentence
    A)   is expressed in the imperative mood.
    B)   is expressed in the indicative mood.
    C)   is expressed in the subjunctive mood.
    D)   uses a correct present participle sequence.

19. "A fire broke out near Dad's chair last night." The preceding sentence   (8j)
    A) uses the passive voice.
    B) uses the active voice.
    C) emphasizes the doer of the action.
    D) both (B) and (C)

20. "The fire was put out by my quick-thinking brother when he   (8j)
    threw a small rug over the flaming waste basket." The
    independent clause in the above sentence
    A) uses the passive voice.
    B) uses the active voice.
    C) emphasizes the doer of the action.
    D) both (B) and (C)

ANSWERS TO MULTIPLE-CHOICE QUESTIONS

1 - D	6 - B	11 - D	16 - B
2 - C	7 - C	12 - B	17 - A
3 - D	8 - D	13 - A	18 - C
4 - A	9 - B	14 - D	19 - D
5 - C	10 - A	15 - D	20 - A

9
CASE OF NOUNS AND PRONOUNS

KEY TERMS AND CONCEPTS

KEY TERMS AND CONCEPTS

case
personal pronoun
person
number
subjective case
objective case
possessive case
compound construction
prepositional phrase

linking verb
interrogative pronoun
relative pronoun
dependent clause
infinitive
gerund
reflexive pronoun
intensive pronoun

FILL-IN QUESTIONS

1. Noun or pronoun _____ refers to changes in   case
   the forms of these words that convey specific
   information about how they relate to other words in
   the sentence. (9)

2. Personal pronouns show changes in first, second and
   third _____ and also indicate whether the   person
   pronoun is singular or plural in _____.   number
   (9)

3. Pronouns in the _____ case ("I," "we,"   subjective
   "she" and "they") function as subjects in a sentence while pronouns in the _____ case   objective
   ("me," "us," "her," and "them") function as objects.
   (9)

4. A _____ construction contains more than   compound
   one subject or object but requires the same pronoun
   case as single constructions. (9a)

5. If you temporarily _____ all of the compound element except the pronoun in question, you will be able to tell which pronoun case is correct. ("Y̶o̶u̶r̶ d̶a̶d̶d̶y̶ a̶n̶d̶ [I] [m̶e̶] love You") (9a)

drop

6. When matching noun and pronoun case, try dropping the _____ following the pronoun to confirm which case is appropriate for the sentence. ("[We] [U̶s̶] taxpayers foot the bill.") (9b)

noun

7. Because a pronoun coming after any linking verb re-names the subject, the pronoun must be in the _____ _____ case, especially in academic writing. (9c)

subjective

8. In the subjective case use the pronouns "who" or "whoever," but in the _____ case use "whom" or "whomever." (9d)

objective

9. When using "than" or "as" in an implied _____ _____, make sure the message is clear by either including all words in the second half of the sentence or mentally filling in the words to check to see if you have chosen the correct pronoun case. (9e)

comparison

10. When a pronoun is the subject or object of an infinitive, use the _____ case. ("He asked me to marry him.") (9f)

objective

11. However, before a gerund use the _____ case. ("His asking so soon surprised me.") (9g)

possessive

12. _____ pronouns reflect back on the subject or object and should not be used as sub-stitutes for subjects or objects. (9h)

Reflexive

MULTIPLE-CHOICE QUESTIONS

1. "With amusement, she stared at the rat running away from him." In the above sentence, "she"
   A) is an object pronoun.
   B) functions as the subject of the sentence.
   C) is a subject pronoun.
   D) both (B) and (C)

(9)

2. In the sample sentence in question #1, "him" is
   A) a direct object.
   B) an indirect object.
   C) the object of a preposition.
   D) both (B) and (C)

(9)

3. "Jill and [I] [me] had given Jack and [they] [them] our   (9a)
   collecting gear." The appropriate pronouns for the above
   sentence are
   A)   me/they.
   B)   me/them.
   C)   I/they.
   D)   I/them.

4. "When Jack and ____ saw the rat, ____ both laughed too."   (9a)
   In the above sentence, the blank spaces
   A)   require subject pronouns.
   B)   require object pronouns.
   C)   could only use "I" and "we" to complete them.
   D)   both (A) and (C)

5. "The water rat dove so quickly that it gave ____ a sur-   (9a)
   prise." In the above sentence, the blank space requires
   A)   a subject pronoun.
   B)   an object pronoun.
   C)   the pronoun "us."
   D)   a possessive pronoun.

6. "But what surprised Jack and ____ most was the rat's large   (9a)
   size." In the above sentence, in order to fill in the
   blank space,
   A)   "him" would be appropriate.
   B)   a subject pronoun is needed.
   C)   "she" would be appropriate.
   D)   both (B) and (C)

7. "[We] [Us] guys had thought that Jill and [they] [them]   (9b)
   would run from the rat." The appropriate pronouns for the
   above sentence are
   A)   Us/they.
   B)   Us/them.
   C)   We/them.
   D)   We/they.

8. "But the problem wasn't [she] [her]; Jill wasn't scared."   (9c)
   The correct pronoun in the above sentence
   A)   follows a linking verb.
   B)   is "her" and not "she."
   C)   comes in the object position in the sentence.
   D)   both (A) and (B)

9. "I don't know [who] [whom] saw Jack slip, but [whoever]   (9d)
   [whomever] it was shouted for help." The correct pronouns
   for the above sentence are
   A)   who/whoever.
   B)   who/whomever.
   C)   whom/whoever.
   D)   whom/whomever.

10. "The campers across the river wondered for [who] [whom] the   (9d)
    help was needed." In the above sentence
    A) we could substitute the pronoun "they" for another.
    B) there are two objects of prepositions.
    C) there is one subject pronoun.
    D) both (B) and (C)

11. "Later I realized that they had been more frightened than   (9e)
    [we] [us]." In the above sentence
    A) "us" is the correct pronoun case.
    B) information is implied.
    C) "than we were frightened" completes the idea.
    D) both (B) and (C)

12. "Yet they expected Raul and [I] [me] to dive in after Jack."   (9f)
    The above sentence
    A) contains an object of an infinitive.
    B) contains a reflexive pronoun.
    C) should have "I" as the correct pronoun case.
    D) contains implied information.

13. "Her jumping in after him surprised even Jack himself." The   (9g)
    above sentence has
    A) an error in pronoun case.
    B) both a gerund and an intensive pronoun.
    C) a reflexive and an intensive pronoun.
    D) both (A) and (C)

14. "After she pulled Jack to the surface, Raul and myself   (9h)
    brought them up on a line." The above sentence contains
    A) an error in pronoun use.
    B) a reflexive pronoun.
    C) an intensive pronoun.
    D) an object of an infinitive.

ANSWERS TO MULTIPLE-CHOICE QUESTIONS

1 - D	5 - B	9 - A	13 - B
2 - C	6 - A	10 - B	14 - A
3 - D	7 - D	11 - D	
4 - A	8 - A	12 - A	

10
PRONOUN
REFERENCE

FILL-IN QUESTIONS

1. For clear communication, a pronoun must refer clearly to single, definite _____. (10a)

   antecedent

2. If the pronoun reference in a passage is ambiguous or confusing, try replacing some of the pronouns with _____, or place the pronouns _____ to their antecedent. (10b)

   nouns
   closer

3. A pronoun cannot have as an antecedent a noun's _____ form, such as "child's." (10c)

   possessive

4. Nor can a pronoun refer to an _____ such as "friendly." (10c)

   adjective

5. In weak writing, the pronouns "this," "that," "which" and _____ are likely not to clearly refer to a specific antecedent. (10c)

   "it"

6. In addition to functioning as a personal pronoun, "it" can be used as an _____, a word that postpones the subject. (10d)

   expletive

7. "It" can also function as part of an idiomatic
   expression of weather, _____ or distance, but   time
   if this pronoun is overused, its three functions can
   become confused.   (10d)

8. In academic writing, the pronoun _____ should be   "you"
   avoided except when directly addressing the reader.
   (10e)

9. When referring to animals, things and sometimes groups
   of people, use "that" with restrictive clauses and
   _____ with nonrestrictive clauses, which should   "which"
   be set off by a comma.   (10f)

10. However, when referring to people, use _____ in both   "who"
    kinds of clauses.   (10f)

MULTIPLE-CHOICE QUESTIONS

1. "Andrew Wyeth did a series of portraits of "Helga, " a   (10b)
    neighbor whom he painted for nearly sixteen years."   In the
    above sentence, the pronoun "whom" has
    A) has a confused antecedent.
    B) "Helga" as its antecedent.
    C) "a neighbor" as its antecedent.
    D) "Andrew Wyeth" as its antecedent.

2. "Wyeth's wife did not know about the paintings of the model (10a)
    for "Helga" because she was very quiet."   In the above
    sentence the pronoun "she" has
    A) an ambiguous antecedent.
    B) "Wyeth's wife as its antecedent.
    C) "Helga" as its antecedent.
    D) both (B) and (C)

3. "Because the model for "Helga" was very quiet, Wyeth's wife (10a)
    did not know about the paintings."   The above sentence is a
    better version of the sample sentence in question #2 because
    A) all pronouns have been eliminated.
    B) the pronouns now have clear antecedents.
    C) "Helga" now comes first in the sentence.
    D) there is no unclear pronoun reference.

4. "Typical of Wyeth's work is his fascination with light play- (10c)
    ing over the surface of a face or a whole human figure."   In
    the above sentence, the pronoun "his" apparently
    A) refers to "Wyeth."
    B) refers to "work."
    C) should be changed to "its."
    D) both (B) and (C)

5. "One painting features a nude, contrasted against a dark   (10c)
    background, seated by a sunlit window; this was entitled

41

'Lovers' by Wyeth's wife." In the above sentence, the pronoun "this" apparently refers
A) to "window."
B) to "background."
C) to "nude."
D) to "painting."

6. "One painting, entitled 'Lovers' by Wyeth's wife, features   (10c)
    a nude, contrasted against a dark background, seated by a
    sunlit window." In the above revision of the sample sen-
    tence in question #5 we see that
    A) the vague pronoun reference has been eliminated.
    B) "painting" is more easily imagined.
    C) the wife suspected an affair.
    D) sentences are clearer without semicolons.

7. "It may be that it was a joke when Betsy Wyeth named it   (10c)
    'Lovers'." In the above sentence the pronoun "it" functions
    as
    A) a personal pronoun.
    B) an expletive.
    C) part of an idiomatic expression.
    D) both (A) and (B)

8. In the sample sentence in question #7, the pronoun "it"   (10d)
    should be
    A) used more precisely.
    B) eliminated completely.
    C) avoided in academic writing.
    D) replaced by "that."

9. "You can imagine the speculation touched off when Wyeth made   (10e)
    public the collection of the "Helga" painting." In the above
    sentence, the pronoun "you" is an example of what is
    A) clearly direct address.
    B) accepted in speech and informal writing.
    C) preferred in formal writing.
    D) both (A) and (C)

10. The "Helga" collection, that was sold for $10 million, was   (10f)
    hidden in an attic of his Pennsylvania farmhouse." The
    above sentence contains
    A) a nonrestrictive clause.
    B) a restrictive clause.
    C) an incorrect pronoun reference.
    D) both (A) and (C)

ANSWERS TO MULTIPLE-CHOICE QUESTIONS

1 - C   4 - D   7 - D   10 - D

2 - A   5 - D   8 - A

3 - D   6 - A   9 - B

11
AGREEMENT

FILL-IN QUESTIONS

1. To communicate clearly, subjects and verbs in
   sentences must "agree" or match in _____   number
   (singular or plural) as well as in _____   person
   (first, second or third). (11)

2. The _____ person (subjects are either "I"   first
   or "we") is the speaker or writer while the
   _____ person (subject is "you") is spoken   second
   or written to. (11)

3. The _____ person is the person or thing   third
   being spoken or written about and the subjects may
   vary widely and include "he," "she," "it," "they"
   and nouns of many kinds. (11)

4. We form most _____ subjects by adding "-s"   plural
   or "-es" except for most pronouns and a few nouns
   that either do not change at all (fish/fish) or
   change significantly in form (goose/geese). (11a)

43

5. Although the special endings attach to plural subjects, not singular ones, we do not add the _____
   _____ endings to simple forms of verbs attached   "-s" or "-es"
   to singular subjects in the third person, present
   tense. (11a)

6. If intervening material such as a prepositional
   phrase separates a subject from its verb in a sentence, temporarily _____ it when you are   ignore
   determining agreement between them. (11b)

7. Use a _____ verb for subjects joined by "and"   plural
   except when the parts combine to form a single person or thing, and when the word "each" or "every"
   precedes two singular subjects connected by "and."
   (11c)

8. When subjects are joined by "or" or "nor," or by
   correlative conjunctions (such as "not only . . .
   but also"), the verb should agree with the subject
   _____ to it. (11d)   closest

9. When sentence word order is inverted and an auxiliary verb or an expletive using "there" or "it"
   (along with the verb "be") _____ the sub-   precedes
   ject, make sure the verb agrees with the subject of
   the sentence. (11e)

10. Most indefinite pronouns (such as "everybody" or
    "nothing") usually require a _____ verb   singular
    although some are plural ("more," "any" or "all")
    depending on the meaning of the sentence. (11f)

11. A _____ noun names a group of people or   collective
    things (such as "family" or "team") and when members
    of this group act as one unit, use a _____   singular
    verb. However, when group members act individually,
    thus creating more than one action, use a plural verb.
    (11g)

12. Although a subject complement may differ in number
    from the subject that it renames, the _____
    verb that attaches them must agree with the subject.   linking
    (11h)

13. Use _____ verbs with subjects that specify   singular
    amounts, as well as with singular subjects that are
    in plural form (such as "jeans") and with titles of
    written works, company names and words used as terms.
    (11j)

14. Since pronouns must match their antecedents in number
    a _____ pronoun is used when "and" joins its   plural
    antecedents. However,when "or" or "nor" joins the

antecedents, the pronoun must agree with the antecedent _____ to it. (11m)   closest

15.   Use a singular pronoun to refer to a collective noun
      when the group acts as one unit, but use a plural
      when the group members act _____.   individually
      (11o)

MULTIPLE-CHOICE QUESTIONS

  1.   "Researchers [tells] [tell] us that AIDS [is] [are] on the   (11a)
       rise in the U.S." In the above sentence
       A)   the subject is plural in both clauses.
       B)   "researchers" is a plural subject.
       C)   "tells" is the correct verb choice.
       D)   both (A) and (B)

  2.   "Often children of an AIDS victim [have] [has] the disease   (11a)
       when they are born." In the above sentence
       A)   "children" is the plural subject.
       B)   "victim" is the singular subject.
       C)   "have" is the correct verb choice.
       D)   both (A) and (C)

  3.   In the sample sentence in question #2, the expression "of   (11b)
       AIDS victims"
       A)   is a prepositional phrase.
       B)   must be considered in determining agreement.
       C)   contains the subject of the sentence.
       D)   both (A) and (B)

  4.   "Dr. Gerald Friedland and his associates at a New York   (11c)
       medical center [treats] [treat] AIDS patients from every
       age group and social class." In the above sentence
       A)   the subject is Friedland.
       B)   "treats" is the correct verb choice.
       C)   a plural verb is needed.
       D)   both (A) and (B)

  5.   The sample sentence in question #4   (11c)
       A)   contains an intervening prepositional phrase.
       B)   has a plural subject connected by "and."
       C)   the parts combine to form a single subject.
       D)   both (A) and (B)

  6.   "Every man and woman in the country now [knows] [know] and   (11c)
       [fears] [fear] the disease." The above sentence
       A)   contains a modal auxiliary.
       B)   requires plural verbs.
       C)   is an exception to the plural subject/plural verb rule.
       D)   both (B) and (C)

7. "Dr. Friedland must [feels] [feel] sad knowing that the
   disease today [has] [have] no cure." In the above sentence
   A) the subjects are both singular.
   B) "feels" and "has" are the correct verb choice.
   C) the first verb follows a modal auxiliary.
   D) both (A) and (C)   (11c)

8. "His research [indicates] [indicate] that casual contact
   does not spread AIDS since neither friends nor family
   members of victims [seems] [seem] to get the disease. The
   dependent clause in the above sentence
   A) has a singular subject.
   B) contains a correlative conjunction.
   C) needs "seems" because of the "either . . . or con-
       struction."
   D) both (B) and (C)   (11d)

9. "There [has] [have] been recent, experimental attempts to
   treat AIDS with alpha interferon." In the above sentence
   A) the auxiliary verb must agree with the subject.
   B) the subject of the sentence is singular.
   C) an expletive construction postpones the subject.
   D) both (A) and (C)   (11e)

10. "Everybody in his medical unit [practices] [practice]
    'Friedland's Law: treat the patient, not the disease,' but
    the staff [applies] [apply] it in their own way." The above
    sentence contains
    A) an indefinite pronoun.
    B) a linking verb.
    C) a collective noun acting as a single unit.
    D) both (A) and (C)   (11f)

11. The correct verb choices for the sentence sample in
    question #10 is
    A) practice/applies.
    B) practice/apply.
    C) practices/applies.
    D) practices/apply.   (11g)

12. "The worst part of Friedland's job [is] [are] the death of
    one of his patients who [has] [have] become a favorite."
    The independent clause in the above sentence contains
    A) a linking verb.
    B) "death" as the singular subject.
    C) a subject complement that renames "worse part."
    D) both (A) and (C)   (11h)

13. The dependent clause in the sample sentence for question #12
    requires
    A) a verb to agree with "patients."
    B) a verb to agree with "who."
    C) a verb to agree with "one."
    D) "have" as the correct verb choice.   (11i)

46

14. "The statistics in a national study [reports] [report] that   (11j)
    five years [is] [are] the longest time an AIDS victim will
    live." In the above sentence the subject
    A) the subject is a course of study.
    B) refers to a body of data.
    C) requires "reports" as the correct verb choice.
    D) both (B) and (C)

15. The dependent clause in the sample sentence for question #14   (11j)
    A) contains a subject that refers to measurement.
    B) contains a plural subject.
    C) requires "is" as the correct verb choice.
    D) both (A) and (C)

16. "High risk groups in several surveys [refers] [refer] to   (11k)
    sexual partners of both male and female AIDS victims as well
    as their infants." The above sentence
    A) contains a plural subject.
    B) uses a word group as a singular term.
    C) requires "refer" as the correct verb choice.
    D) both (B) and (C)

17. "Each of the victims [finds] [find] an outlet for [his]   (11l)
    [their] feelings when caseworkers or Friedland himself
    [leads] [lead] the support groups." In the independent
    clause of the above sentence
    A) the plural subject requires a plural verb.
    B) "their" is the correct pronoun choice.
    C) "finds" is the correct verb choice.
    D) both (B) and (C)

18. The dependent clause in the sample sentence for question #17   (11m)
    requires the verb
    A) to agree with "Friedland."
    B) to agree with "caseworkers."
    C) to agree with a plural subject.
    D) both (B) and (C)

19. Refer back to the sample sentence for question #10. In   (11o)
    this sentence the "their"
    A) refers to a collective noun.
    B) refers to a group of people acting as a single unit.
    C) is an error in pronoun agreement.
    D) both (A) and (B)

ANSWERS TO MULTIPLE-CHOICE QUESTIONS

1 – B	6 – C	11 – C	16 – B
2 – D	7 – D	12 – D	17 – C
3 – A	8 – B	13 – C	18 – A
4 – C	9 – D	14 – B	19 – A
5 – D	10 – A	15 – D	

12
DISTINGUISHING BETWEEN ADJECTIVES AND ADVERBS

KEY TERMS AND CONCEPTS

adjective
adverb
modifier
verb
double negative
contraction
linking verb
subject complement
positive

comparative form
superlative form
double comparative
double superlative
irregular adjective/adverb
less/fewer
nouns as modifiers

FILL-IN QUESTIONS

1. Adjectives and adverbs function as _____,   modifiers
   words or groups of words that describe or clarify the
   meaning of other words. (12a)

2. Although inexperienced writers may mistakenly inter-
   change adjective and adverbs, we can avoid this if we
   understand that they modify _____ kinds   different
   of words. (12a)

3. Use only _____ to modify verbs, adjectives   verbs
   and other adverbs. (12b)

4. Now considered nonstandard, a _____ negative   double
   is a statement that contains two negative modifiers.
   (12c)

5. Since linking verbs rename or describe the subject
   (usually a noun or pronoun), the subject complement
   must be an _____. (12d)   adjective

6. Thus, only the _____ "bad" is correct when verbs such as "felt" are used as linking verbs. (12d)

adjective

7. "Good" is always an adjective; "well" is an _____ _____ when referring to good health, but is an _____ when describing any action other than those relating to health. (12d)

adjective

adverb

8. Most adjectives and adverbs show degrees of intensity by adding "-er" or _____ or else by combining with the words "more" or "most" depending on the number of _____ the modifier contains. (12e)

"-est"

syllables

9. With _____ of two or more syllables, "more" or "most" are used, but with adjectives of two syllables, the practice varies. (12e)

adverbs

10. Two-syllables adjectives ending in "-y" take the "-er" or "-est" form after changing the "-y" to ____. (12e)

"-i"

11. "Less" refers to amounts or values that form one whole while "fewer" refers to numbers or anything that can be _____. (12e)

counted

12. When too many nouns pile up as modifiers, a writer can revise to clarify by rewriting the sentence as well as by changing a noun to its adjective form or to its _____ case. (12f)

possessive

MULTIPLE-CHOICE QUESTIONS

1. "A very patient man, Edmund Halley struggled tirelessly to make Issac Nerton's work of immense genius, Principia Mathematica, known to the world." In the above sentence, the term "tirelessly"   (12a)
   A) is an "-ly" adjective.
   B) modifies "Halley."
   C) modifies "struggled."
   D) both (A) and (C)

2. In the sample sentence for question #1, the term "work" is   (12a)
   A) a verb modified by "of immense genius."
   B) a noun modified by "Issac Newton's."
   C) a noun modified by "of immense genius."
   D) both (B) and (C)

3. In the sample sentence for question #1, the term "very" is   (12b)
   A) an adjective that modifies "man."
   B) an adverb that modifies "Edmund Halley."
   C) an adjective that modifies an adverb.
   D) an adverb that modifies "patient."

4. "Halley's fascination with comets greatly interested him in   (12a)
    Newton's explanation of the gravitational pull of the sun on
    other heavenly bodies." In the sample sentence above, the
    terms "greatly" and "heavenly"
    A) are both adjectives modifying nouns.
    B) are both adverbs that end in "ly."
    C) are an adverb and an adjective respectively.
    D) are an adjective and an adverb respectively.

5. "Sir Robert Hook jealously claimed that Newton hadn't never   (12c)
    solved the problem of celestial motion." In the above
    sentence
    A) the term "jealously" should be "most jealous."
    B) there is a nonstandard double negative.
    C) "jealously" modifies "Sir Robert Hook."
    D) both (B) and (C)

6. "Newton grew reluctant to publish his work because he was   (12d)
    assuredly that others might steal his ideas." In the above
    sentence, "assuredly" is an error because
    A) "was" is a linking verb.
    B) it should be an adverb.
    C) it should take a complement (adjective) form.
    D) both (A) and (C)

7. Another linking verb in the sample sentence for question #6   (12d)
    is
    A) grew
    B) publish
    C) steal
    D) none of the above

8. "Although he had less genius, Halley's good natured gre-   (12e)
    gariousness contrasted sharply with Newton's arrogant
    reclusiveness and dark moods." In the sentence the term
    "less"
    A) refers to numbers or anything that can be counted.
    B) refers to amounts or values that form one whole.
    C) is the comparative form of "little."
    D) both (B) and (C)

9. "Halley felt badly after his father's murder, but he assisted   (12d)
    Newton well by paying for the publication of Principia himself
    although Newton was wealthier." In the above sentence the term
    "badly"
    A) follows an action verb.
    B) is correct as an adverb modifying "felt."
    C) should be "bad" as a complement to "Halley."
    D) both (A) and (B)

10. In the sample sentence for question #9, the term "wealthier"   (12e)
    A) should be "more wealthy" since it is an adverb.
    B) requires changing a "-y" to an "-i" spelling.
    C) derives from an adjective of two syllables.
    D) both (B) and (C)

11. In the sample sentence for question #9. the term "well" (12d)
   A) should be changed to "good."
   B) modifies "Newton" as an adjective.
   C) modifies "assisted" as an adverb.
   D) both (A) and (B)

12. "Because Hook was Britain's Royal Society president, they (12f)
   had declined to print one of the most greatest books ever
   written." In the above sentence the reader would have an
   easier time if
   A) "Britain's" were changed from the possessive case to an
      adjective form.
   B) "Britain's" was in a prepositional phrase.
   C) no nouns were used as modifiers.
   D) both (A) and (C)

13. In the sample sentence for question #12, the term "greatest"
   A) cannot modify only "one."
   B) is part of a double comparative.
   C) is part of a double superlative.
   D) should be "most great" instead.

ANSWERS TO THE MULTIPLE-CHOICE QUESTIONS

1 - C	5 - B	8 - D	11 - C
2 - D	6 - D	9 - C	12 - B
3 - D	7 - A	10 - D	13 - C
4 - C			

13
SENTENCE FRAGMENTS

KEY TERMS AND CONCEPTS

sentence fragment
complete sentence
verb
subject
imperative statement
clause
independent clause
dependent clause
subordinating word
subordinating conjunction

relative pronoun
verbal phrase
prepositional phrase
appositive
intentional fragment
compound predicate

FILL-IN QUESTIONS

1. A sentence fragment is merely part of a sentence
   that has been punctuated as if it were a _____   complete
   _____ sentence. (13a)

2. You can test to discover and eliminate fragments by
   checking to see if the word group has a subject and
   a complete _____. (13a)   verb

3. Verbs convey information about what is happening,
   has happened, or will happen, so check to make sure
   the supposed verb can change _____ to com-   form
   municate a change in time. (13a)

4. Fragments sometimes should have, or be attached to,
   the subject of the sentence _____ or   preceding
   following them. (13a)

5. To make sure the sentence has a subject, identify
    it by using the verb in a question beginning with
    "who" or _____. (13a)   "what"

6. Even if the word group has a subject and verb, it
    still is a fragment if it begins with a subordi-
    nating word and lacks an _____   independent
    clause to complete the thought. (13a)

7. The words "after," "although," "because," "if,"
    "when," etc. are called subordinating _____   conjunctions
    _____ when they join a dependent clause
    to an independent one. (13a)

8. The words "who," "which," "that," etc. are called
    _____ pronouns when they join a depend-   relative
    ent clause to an independent one. (13a)

9. Verbal phrases, prepositional phrases, appositives
    and other word groups that are fragments in them-
    selves can either be _____ to become   rewritten
    independent clauses or can be _____ to   joined
    independent clauses that come before or after them.
    (13c)

10. Occasionally, professional writers _____   intentionally
    use fragments for emphasis or effects, but the ability
    to discriminate when they are appropriate comes only
    with well-developed writing skill and experience.
    (13d)

MULTIPLE-CHOICE QUESTIONS

1. "Today suntans have become popular. Perhaps signifying   (13a)
    'tennis at the club' instead of 'field hand.'" The first
    word group.
    A) is a dependent clause.
    B) has a subject and a verb.
    C) is an independent clause.
    D) both (B) and (C)

2. The second word group in the sample for question #1   (13c)
    A) has "tennis" as the subject.
    B) lacks only a subject.
    C) is a dependent clause.
    D) is a verbal phrase.

3. "Because extensive exposure to the sun begins a cumulative,   (13a)
    irreversible and damaging process. Dermatologists believe
    it may lead to skin cancer." The first word group in the
    above
    A) has "exposure" for its subject.
    B) is an independent clause.

54

C) has "process" for its verb.
D) both (A) and (C)

4. The first word group in the sample for question #3   (13b)
   A) should be connected to the clause following it.
   B) is not a clause.
   C) is a complete sentence.
   D) both (A) and (B)

5. "The changes in life style reflected in the change in sta-   (13a)
   tistics. The risk of dangerous melanoma gone up 900 percent
   since 1930." The word groups above
   A) should be joined to create a complete sentence.
   B) both lack complete verbs.
   C) should be revised by adding words.
   D) both (B) and (C)

6. "In addition to causing skin cancer. Sun exposure ages the   (13c)
   skin as well." The first word group in the above
   A) is a dependent clause.
   B) is an independent clause.
   C) is a phrase.
   D) needs added words to join it to the following sentence.

7. "One form of 'shade' now available is sunblock. Lotions or   (13c)
   creams containing PABA, which absorbs ultraviolet radiation."
   In the word groups above
   A) the first is a fragment.
   B) the second is a fragment.
   C) both are fragments.
   D) neither is a fragment.

8. The second word group in the sample for question #7 is   (13c)
   A) a prepositional phrase.
   B) an appositive.
   C) a dependent clause.
   D) a verbal phrase.

9. "A doctor who has treated hundreds of sun related skin prob-   (13c)
   lems is blunt in his advice. 'Stay out of the sun.'" The
   term "who" in the first word group above
   A) is a relative pronoun.
   B) is a type of subordinating word.
   C) is part of a compound predicate.
   D) both (A) and (B)

10. The second word group in the sample in question #9   (13a)
    A) is a dependent clause.
    B) lacks a subject.
    C) is an imperative with an implied subject.
    D) lacks a verb.

ANSWERS TO MULTIPLE-CHOICE QUESTIONS

1 – D	4 – A	7 – B	10 – C
2 – D	5 – D	8 – B	
3 – A	6 – C	9 – D	

14

COMMA SPLICES AND FUSED SENTENCES

KEY TERMS AND CONCEPTS

comma splice (comma fault)
fused sentence (run-on sentence)
independent clause
conjunctive adverb
transitional expression
coordinating conjunction

compound sentence
complex sentence
dependent clause
subordinating conjunction
relative pronoun

FILL-IN QUESTIONS

1. A comma splice occurs when only a comma is used to join two _____ clauses. (14a)

independent

2. When two independent clauses are not separated by any punctuation or are not joined by a comma with a coordinating conjunction, the result is a _____ sentence. (14a)

fused

3. An independent clause, which contains both a _____ and a predicate, can stand alone as an independent grammatical unit of meaning. (14a)

subject

4. You can use a period to separate independent clauses, or use a _____ for those clauses closely related in meaning. (14b)

semicolon

5. The ideas in independent clauses that are closely related and grammatically equivalent can be joined ed with a _____ conjunction (such as "and," "but" or "so") preceded by a comma, to create a compound sentence. (14c)

coordinating

6. When one idea can be logically subordinated to the other, another option in correcting comma splices is to create a _____ sentence by revising one of the independent clauses into a dependent one. (14d)

complex

7. The subordinating _____ must fit the meaning of the sentence; for example, "as" or "because" signal reason, "although" signals concession, "if" signals condition, and "before" or "when" signal _____ relationships. (14d)

conjunction

time

8. Relative pronouns such as "who," "which" and "that" can also begin _____ clauses, which cannot stand alone but must be attached to independent clauses. (14d)

dependent

9. Independent clauses do stand alone; however, avoid creating a comma _____ by joining them merely with a conjunctive adverb. (14e)

splice

10. A semicolon should _____ either a conjunctive adverb or transitional words. In fact, a period can precede either of them, but in both cases they should be followed immediately by a _____. (14e)

precede

comma

MULTIPLE-CHOICE QUESTIONS

1. "Some parents expect their children to be little adults,   (14a)
   they confuse an adult-like vocabulary and information with
   intelligence." In the above construction there
   A) are two independent clauses.
   B) is one dependent and one independent clause.
   C) is a comma splice
   D) both (A) and (B)

2. The subject/verb pairs in the sample construction for   (14a)
   question #1 are
   A) parents/expect and children/to be.
   B) parents/expect and they/confuse.
   C) children/to be and adults/confuse.
   D) none of the above

3. The comma splice in the sample construction for question   (14b)
   #1 can be corrected by
   A) inserting a period after "adults" and capitalizing
       "they."
   B) inserting a semicolon between "adults" and "they."
   C) adding "when" in front of "some parents."
   D) all of the above

4. "We must respect the fact that play is a child's work, the play is the learning." To correct the comma splice in the above construction (14d)
   A) a coordinating conjunction should precede the comma.
   B) a subordinating conjunction should precede "fact."
   C) a subordinating conjunction could precede "the play."
   D) a coordinating conjunction could replace "that."

5. The cause of the comma splice in the above construction is probably that (14a)
   A) the second independent clause starts with a pronoun.
   B) a conjunctive adverb occurs within it.
   C) an explanation follows the first independent clause.
   D) transitional material interrupts the two clauses.

6. "Children who use right brain functions develop their intuitive, imaginative and spatial abilities, however they often do less well in the traditional classroom than less fidgety, verbally oriented children." In the above construction the writer should (14e)
   A) replace the comma after "abilities" with a semicolon.
   B) insert a comma after "however."
   C) insert a period after "however."
   D) both (A) and (B)

7. The cause of the comma splice in the sample construction for question #6 is probably that (14a)
   A) the second independent clause starts with a pronoun.
   B) a conjunctive adverb follows the first independent clause.
   C) an example follows the first independent clause.
   D) both (A) and (B)

8. The subject/verb pairs in the sample construction for question #6 are (14a)
   A) children/use and they/do.
   B) children/develop and they/do.
   C) who/use and they/fidget.
   D) none of the above

9. "Some may not realize that between the ages of four and seven, children learn best through fantasy, physical activity and storytelling for example, Mike's father thinks his having a imaginary playmate is weird." The cause of the fused sentence in the above construction is probably that (14a)
   A) the second independent clause starts with a pronoun.
   B) a transition follows the first independent clause.
   C) an example follows the first independent clause.
   D) both (B) and (C)

10. One of the best ways to correct the fused sentence in the sample for question #9 would be to add (14e)

A) a semicolon before "for example."
B) "because" before the word "some."
C) "who" after "Mike's father."
D) a comma and a coordinating conjunction after "story-telling."

ANSWERS TO MULTIPLE-CHOICE QUESTIONS

1 - D	4 - C	7 - D	10 - A
2 - B	5 - C	8 - B	
3 - D	6 - D	9 - D	

15
SENTENCES THAT SEND UNCLEAR MESSAGES

KEY TERMS AND CONCEPTS

unnecessary shift
consistency in person
consistency in number
shifts in subject
passive voice
active voice
consistency in tense
consistency in mood
indirect discourse
direct discourse
modifiers

misplaced modifiers
ambiguous placement
squinting modifiers
wrong placement
awkward placement
split infinitive
dangling modifier
mixed construction
faulty predication
incomplete sentences
elliptical constructions

1. Many sentence errors escape correction in proofreading because the brain unconsciously corrects errors or fills in _____ material. (15)   missing

2. One way to avoid the above problem is to finish your writing assignment well ahead of time so that you can _____ again later with a more objective state of mind.   (15)   proofread

3. Inconsistency in person and number commonly occurs when a writer shifts to the second-person _____   "you"
    _____ from the first-person "I" or from a third person noun; however, the second person should be used only when directly addressing the _____.   reader
    (15a)

4. Unnecessary shifts in subject and voice can occur when the writer moves from the active voice, which

emphasizes the doer of the action, to the _____ _____ voice, which focuses on the object receiving the action.   (15a)   passive

5. If verb tense change is illogical in a sentence, its ability to convey information about _____ _____ connections will be confused.   (15a)   time

6. The most common mood error is a shift between the indicative (a statement or question) and the _____ (a command or request).   (15a)   imperative

7. Any shift between indirect and direct discourse should be indicated by _____ marks and other material.   (15a)   quotation

8. A _____ modifier is descriptive information incorrectly positioned in the sentence so that it confuses meaning.   (15b)   misplaced

9. Ambiguous placement and squinting modifiers both confusion because they can _____ or describe more than one idea within the same sentence.   (15b)   modify

10. Awkward placements _____ the smooth flow of a sentence and occur when intervening material is inserted between the "to" and its verb in an infinitive, between the subject and verb, or within the group of words that comprise a verb phrase.   (15b)   interrupt

11. A dangling modifier can be corrected by revising so that the intended subject is expressed rather than _____ and placed adjacent to the modifying expression.   (15c)   implied

12. Mixed _____, which are sometimes caused by the phrase "the fact that," start out taking one grammatical form and then _____ _____ to another, thus creating a mixed sentence with two parts that do not make sense together.   (15d)   constructions

change

13. Illogical or faulty predication is a type of mixed sentence that often begins with "is when" or "is _____"; thus, such expressions should be avoided in formal writing.   (15d)   where

14. In _____ constructions, the words that are left out must be exactly the same as the words that appear in the sentence.   (15e)   elliptical

15. To make comparisons complete, unambiguous and
    logical, include all words needed to make clear
    the _____ between the items or ideas   relationship
    being compared. (15e)

MULTIPLE-CHOICE QUESTIONS

1. "I was looking forward to seeing Halley's Comet, but when   (15a)
   it came you could hardly see it in the southern sky." The
   above sentence lacks consistency in
   A) person
   B) number
   C) subject
   D) voice

2. "When midnight viewers saw the comet in 1910, a brilliant   (15a)
   display was observed." The above sentence shifts
   A) from first-person to second-person.
   B) subjects from "viewers" to "display."
   C) from singular to plural.
   D) from indirect to direct discourse.

3. The sample sentence for question #2 also contains an   (15a)
   unnecessary shift
   A) from imperative to subjunctive mood.
   B) from past to present tense.
   C) from active to passive voice.
   D) to a third-person pronoun.

4. "As the comet moved across the sky back in 1910, our neigh-   (15a)
   bor woke us up to ask was it the end of the world." In the
   above sentence, there is an unmarked shift from
   A) direct discourse to indirect discourse.
   B) indirect discourse to direct discourse.
   C) indicative to imperative mood.
   D) both (B) and (C)

5. "No matter what direction the comet is coming from, always   (15b)
   pointing away from the sun, the tail stretches long and
   luminous." In the above sentence
   A) a squinting modifier causes ambiguity.
   B) there is a shift in verb tense.
   C) either "comet" or "tail" could be modified by "always
       pointing away from the sun."
   D) both (A) and (C)

6. "The interaction of the comet with solar winds made of   (15b)
   hydrogen blowing constantly through the solar system
   creates the gaseous tail." The above sentence contains an
   awkwardly placed modifier that
   A) splits an infinitive.

63

B) interrupts a subject and verb.
C) interrupts a verb phrase.
D) creates ambiguity.

7. "When near enough to the sun to be illuminated, we see   (15c)
    only a tiny percentage of those comets thought to exist."
    In the above sentence
    A) "we" is the correct subject of the dependent clause.
    B) "sun" is the correct subject of the dependent clause.
    C) an intended subject is not stated.
    D) the writer's brain is missing.

8. The error in the sample sentence for question #7   (15c)
    A) is a dangling modifier.
    B) involves awkward placement within a verb phrase.
    C) is caused by ambiguous placement.
    D) both (A) and (B)

9. "Because Halley's Comet was approaching, the fact that Sam   (15d)
    Houston defeated Santa Ana in 1835 caused the birth of the
    Republic of Texas." The above sentence contains an example
    of
    A) a dangling modifier.
    B) mixed constructions.
    C) ambiguous placement.
    D) an unnecessary shift from active to passive.

10. "Its orbit around the sun is when most people can view a   (15d)
    comet." The problem with the above sentence is
    A) faulty predication.
    B) an illogical connection between subject and object.
    C) that the complement should rename "orbit."
    D) both (A) and (C)

11. "Halley's Comet made one famous return in 451 A.D. after the (15e)
    defeat of Attila the Hun, and in 1066 and 1222, coinciding
    with the conquests of William of Normandy and Genghis Khan."
    In the above sentence the elliptical construction
    A) correctly omits unnecessary words.
    B) is a mixed constructions.
    C) incorrectly omits "other famous returns."
    D) has an unnecessary use of the passive voice.

12. "The comet was brighter in 1910 because it was several   (15e)
    million miles nearer as it passed the earth." The compari-
    son in the above sentence
    A) is incomplete.
    B) is ambiguous.
    C) is illogical.
    D) has an incomplete intensifier.

13. "Radio astronomy, one of major technologies developed since   (15e)
    1910, has yielded valuable data on the chemical composition
    of the nucleus and tail." In the above sentence,
    A) a comparison in ambiguous.
    B) an article has been omitted.
    C) an elliptical construction omits unnecessary words.
    D) awkward placement interrupts the flow of the sentence.

ANSWERS TO MULTIPLE-CHOICE QUESTIONS

1 - A   5 - D   9 - B   13 - B

2 - B   6 - B   10 - D

3 - C   7 - C   11 - C

4 - B   8 - A   12 - A

16
CONCISENESS

KEY TERMS AND CONCEPTS

conciseness
expletive
active voice
passive voice
elleptical construction

strong verb
weak verb
nominal
padding ("deadwood")

FILL-IN QUESTIONS

1. _____ writing is direct and to the point   Concise
   as it clearly delivers its message; thus, it helps
   keep the reader's interest. (16)

2. Often confusing and irritating to readers, _____,   wordy
   indirect writing forces them to clear away _____   unnecessary
   _____ words and also seems abstract and uninterest-
   ing. (16a)

3. Coming before the subject in a sentence, an _____   expletive
   postpones the subject and weakens its impact by adding
   "it" or "there" to a form of the verb "be." (16a)

4. Sentences seem more lively and concise when they use
   the _____ voice (with focus on the subject as   active
   doer of the action. (16a)

5. Writers using the _____ voice sometimes name   passive
   the doer of the action (in a phrase that starts with
   "by") but often leave it out entirely; however, they
   should avoid hiding important _____, no   information
   matter how "objective" the sentence may sound. (16a)

6. To achieve clarity and conciseness, often writers can
    _____ sentences or they can _____   combine
    a clause to a phrase or a phrase to a single word.   reduce
    (16a)

7. Choosing _____ verbs instead of weak ones (such   strong
    as forms of "be" and "have") will more directly convey
    action and thus have greater impact as well as reducing
    wordiness. (16a)

8   When some writers attempt to write "formally" they some-
    times load their sentences down with _____   "deadwood"
    or padding--empty words and phrases that do not sub-
    stitute for more ideas or more evidence. (16b)

9. "As a matter of _____," because these expressions   fact
    contain little originality or thought, you can spot
    deadwood if you can automatically fill in these blanks
    and see "the _____ I am trying to make". (16b)   point

10. While planned repetition can create a powerful rhythmic
    effect, unplanned repetition or _____ can   redundancy
    create dull, awkward and wordy writing. (16c)

MULTIPLE-CHOICE QUESTIONS

1. Which of the following contains an unnecessary expletive   (16a)
    construction
    A) "Encore!" a man yelled.
    B) There was a man yelling "Encore!".
    C) A man yelled "Encore!".
    D) none of the above

2. "As she ended the show, the magician was greeted by the   (16a)
    children's joyous laughter." The above sentence
    A) uses the active voice in the main clause.
    B) omits information about the doer of the action.
    C) contains a passive construction.
    D) both (B) and (C)

3. "Her assistant had been suspended so that he appeared to   (16a)
    be floating in thin air." The above sentence
    A) uses the active voice in the main clause.
    B) omits information about the doer of the action.
    C) contains a passive construction.
    D) both (B) and (C)

4. Original: "The Magnifica had been dressed in a black tux. (16a)
    When she waved the flaming red cape, the clothing had been
    transformed into a white feather dress.
    Revision: "Waving the flaming red cape, the Magnifica trans-
    formed her black tux into a white feather dress." In the
    above revision

A) a clause is reduced to a phrase.
B) a passive construction is changed to an active one.
C) sentences are combined.
D) all of the above

5. Original: "People who are always cynical look down on such (16a) 'magic', but children and those who are young at heart love it."
   Revision: "Cynics look down on such 'magic', but children of all ages love it." In the above revision
   A) clauses have been reduced to phrases and words.
   B) phrases have been reduced to words.
   C) strong verbs have replaced weak ones.
   D) unnecessary passives have been eliminated.

6. Original: "Some illusionists, such as Houdini, have caused (16a) fascination for generations."
   Revision: "Some illusionists, such as Houdini, have fascinated generations." The above revision
   A) reduces a clause into a phrase.
   B) turns a nominal back into a verb.
   C) eliminates a passive construction for an active one.
   D) both (B) and (C)

7. "But in a very real sense the nature of Magnifica's magic (16b) was its manner of engineering, involving her assistants hidden in the floor and ceiling." The above sentence could best be made more clear and concise by
   A) eliminating "deadwood."
   B) turning a nominal back into a verb.
   C) revising redundancies.
   D) reducing clauses to phrases or words.

8. "The feather dress, for example, was actually a screen held (16c) up from below by an assistant standing under the stage beneath Magnifica above him." The above sentence could best be made more clear and concise by
   A) eliminating "deadwood."
   B) turning nominal back into a verb
   C) revising redundancies.
   D) reducing clauses to phrases or words.

9. Original: "Because they were pleased, the children sur- (16c) rounded the Magnifica in a delighted circle."
   Revised: "Delighted, the children surrounded the Magnifica."
   The above revision
   A) reduces a clause.
   B) eliminates redundancy.
   C) eliminates "deadwood" expressions.
   D) both (A) and (B)

10. "Her special magic--the Magnifica's love of children-- (16b) attracted even those who approached her in a shy manner."
    We can revise the above sentence for concise wording by

68

A) changing the last phrase to "shyly."
B) changing the pronoun "those" to "children."
C) replacing the last eight word with "shy one."
D) either (A) or (C)

ANSWERS TO MULTIPLE-CHOICE QUESTIONS

1 - B   4 - D   7 - A   10 - D

2 - C   5 - A   8 - C

3 - D   6 - B   9 - D

17
COORDINATION AND SUBORDINATION

KEY TERMS AND CONCEPTS

compound (coordinate) sentence
coordinating conjunction
independent clause
dependent clause
complex clause

subordinating conjunction
adverb clause
relative pronoun
adjective clause
compound-complex sentence

FILL-IN QUESTIONS

1. _____ uses grammatical equivalents to   Coordination
   express a balance or sequence of ideas, so sentences
   of this type usually have two independent parts
   equally weighted in importance. (17a)

2. In contrast, _____ suggests a relation-   subordination
   ship between two ideas where one is less important
   or is dependent on the other. (17d)

3. A semicolon or a coordinating _____ such   conjunction
   as "and," "but," "or" and "yet" (following a comma)
   joined two independent clauses in a compound sentence. (17)

4. Coordination and subordination usually suggest
   _____ among ideas more effectively than a   relationships
   group of shorter separate sentences. (17d)

5. However, coordination is _____ and   illogical
   confusing when the ideas in each part of the compound
   are not related to each other.   (17c)

6. When writers _____ coordination, they may   overuse
   fail to effectively relate their ideas to one another
   in their sentences or they may create wordy, monotonous "babble".   (17c)

7. Sentences using subordination contain an _____   independent
   _____ clause, which stands on its own as a complete grammatical unit, and a _____ clause   dependent
   clause which cannot stand alone as a sentence.   (17c)

8. Adverb clauses begin with _____ conjunctions   subordinating
   such as "after," "until," "if" or "although" and
   usually occur before or after the independent clause.
   (17c)

9. Adjective clauses begin with _____ pronouns   relative
   such as "who," "which," or "that" and usually either
   interrupt or follow the independent clause the modify.
   (17c)

10. When a sentence contains a nonrestrictive _____   adjective
    _____ clause, which modifies but is not essential to
    the meaning of the sentence, use _____ to   commas
    separate it from the independent clause.   (17c)

11. Using a variety of sentence structures rather than
    _____ of subordination can avoid con-   overuse
    fusing, illogical sentences and make clear the key
    points and relationship among ideas.   (17f)

12. Compound-_____ sentences combine coordi-   complex
    nation with subordination.   (17g)

MULTIPLE-CHOICE QUESTIONS

1. "Loggerhead sea turtles have been nesting in record numbers   (17)
   but this endangered species is not necessarily making a
   come back." The above sentence
   A) is compound.
   B) contains a coordinating conjunction.
   C) contains two independent clauses.
   D) all of the above

2. The sentence in question #1   (17)
   A) needs two commas to set off the balancing clause.
   B) should have a comma following "species."
   C) should have a comma preceding "but."
   D) is correctly punctuated.

71

3. "Lights along the beach deter turtles from coming ashore to   (17a)
   nest and keep hatchlings from finding their way to the sea."
   The above sentence
   A)   is compound.
   B)   contains two independent clauses.
   C)   has only one subject.
   D)   all of the above

4. The sentence sample in question #3   (17c)
   A)   contains two verbs within the same clause.
   B)   needs a comma to precede "and."
   C)   overuses coordination.
   D)   contains ideas that are not logically related.

5. "If a mother is killed it takes twenty years for her hatch-   (17d)
   lings to mature and return to lay eggs." The above sentence
   A)   is compound.
   B)   contains a dependent clause.
   C)   contains two independent clauses.
   D)   both (A) and (C)

6. The sentence sample in question #5   (17c)
   A)   needs a comma after "killed."
   B)   contains a subordinating conjunction.
   C)   is correctly punctuated.
   D)   both (A) and (B)

7. "Some shrimp fishermen voluntarily use nets that automati-   (17c)
   cally release the turtles and other larger sea creatures."
   The above sentence
   A)   contains an adjective clause.
   B)   contains an adverb clause.
   C)   contains a subordinating conjunction.
   D)   both (A) and (C)

8. The expression beginning with "that" in the sentence sample   (17c)
   in question #7
   A)   is nonrestrictive and simply modifies "nets."
   B)   needs to be set off with commas.
   C)   restricts the meaning of "nets."
   D)   both (A) and (B)

9. "Conservationists who collect and hatch the eggs release the   (17g)
   turtles, but many still drown in the shrimpers' nets." The
   above sentence
   A)   contains an adverb clause.
   B)   is compound.
   C)   is complex.
   D)   both (B) and (C)

10. In the sentence sample in question #9, the term "conserva-   (17d)
    tionists" is
    A)   modified by an adjective clause.
    B)   antecedent of the pronoun "many."

C) the subject of an independent clause.
D) both (A) and (C)

11. "Although night beach driving is now banned, hotels should   (17g)
     shield their lights since they disturb nesting mothers and
     hatchlings." The above sentence contains
     A) two independent clauses.
     B) an adjective clause and an adverb clause.
     C) two adverb clauses.
     D) two adjectives clauses.

12. In the sentence sample in question #11, the term "although"   (17c)
     shows a subordinate relationship of
     A) concession.
     B) condition.
     C) reason.
     D) time limit.

ANSWERS TO MULTIPLE-CHOICE QUESTIONS

1 - D   4 - A   7 - A   10 - D

2 - C   5 - B   8 - C   11 - C

3 - C   6 - D   9 - D   12 - A

18
PARALLELISM

KEY TERMS AND CONCEPTS

parallelism
equivalent grammatical form
faulty parallelism
climactic order
balanced sentence
coordinating conjunction
correlative conjunction

FILL-IN QUESTIONS

1. Parallelism involves the use of _____   equivalent
    grammatical forms to express similar ideas and informa-
    tion; words, phrases and clauses in parallel structures
    thus must occur in the _____ form (e.g. both verbs   same
    present tense).   (18a)

2. Using parallel structures in your writing can add
    strength of expression, impact and _____.   grace
    (18)

3. Deliberate repetition of words or groups of words
    create a _____ that emphasizes your meaning.   rhythm
    (18a)

4. Especially effective are parallel elements arranged
    from least to most important or in _____   climactic
    order.   (18b)

5. The impact of compared or contrasted ideas can be
    enhanced when expressed in _____ sentences.   balanced
    (18b)

6. Use parallel constructions whenever your words, phrases or clauses are joined together _____ _____ conjunctions (such as "and," "but," "or" and "so"). (18c)

coordinating

7. When you link sentence elements, use parallel constructions with paired words or _____ conjunctions (such as "both . . . and," "not only . . . but also," "either . . . or") as well as with clause openers (such as "who . . . and who"). (18c)

correlative

8. Repeating propositions, _____ (such as "a," "an" and "the") as well as the "to" of the infinitive can enhance the effect of parallels. (18c)

articles

9. In longer passages of writing or speaking, use parallel sentences and controlled repetition of words, concepts and rhythm for greater _____ and impact. (18d)

unity

10. Formally written lists and outlines will _____ _____ their information more subtly, clearly and forcefully if they appear in parallels. (18e)

communicate

MULTIPLE-CHOICE QUESTIONS

1. "The worthless and offensive members of society invariably think themselves the most ill-used people alive". The above sentence (18a)
    A) contains some equivalent grammatical forms.
    B) uses controlled repetition.
    C) contains balanced clauses.
    D) both (A) and (C)

2. The sentence sample in question #1 (18a)
    A) has no parallel structure.
    B) uses parallel adjectives.
    C) uses parallel verbs.
    D) has parallel subject/verb combinations.

3. "We are all wise in capacity, though so few in energy" The parallels in the above sentence (18c)
    A) emphasize a contrast.
    B) repeat preposition/noun phrases.
    C) use parallel subjects
    D) both (A) and (B)

4. "The greatest genius is the most indebted man." The above sentence uses (18b)
    A) no parallel patterns.
    B) deliberate repetition for emphasis.
    C) parallel modifier/noun constructions.
    D) both (B) and (C)

5. "He [Shakespeare] loves virtue, not for its obligations, but   (18b)
    for its grace; he delights in the world, in man, in woman,
    for the lovely light that sparkles from them." The above
    sentence uses parallel
    A) prepositional phrases.
    B) grammatically equivalent verbs.
    C) climactic order.
    D) both (A) and (B)

6. The sample sentence in question #5 achieves impact and rhythm   (18b)
    through repeated
    A) articles and infinitives.
    B) phrase patterns.
    C) sound patterns (especially "l" and "g").
    D) both (B) and (C)

7. "The superior [skeptical] mind will find itself equally at   (18b)
    odds with the evils of society and with the projects that
    are offered to relieve them." The above sentence uses
    A) phrases joined by a coordinating conjunction.
    B) clauses joined by a coordinating conjunction.
    C) clauses joined by a correlative conjunction.
    D) none of the above

8. "The actor responds to critics both by quietly withdrawing   (18c)
    from them and with angry confrontations." The above sen-
    tence attempts to
    A) use parallel nouns.
    B) link elements with a correlative conjunction.
    C) use parallel prepositional phrases.
    D) use parallel adjectives.

9. The sample sentence in question #8 could best be revised by   (18c)
    rewriting the last part to read:
    A) "both by quiet withdrawal and by angry confrontation."
    B) "both by quietly withdrawing from them and by angrily
        confronting them."
    C) either (A) or (B)
    D) neither (A) or (B)

10. "We have to thank researchers for [reconstructing] the   (18b)
    stage which Shakespeare altered, remodeled and finally
    made his own." In the above sentence, the parallel
    elements
    A) use clause beginners.
    B) move from the least to most important.
    C) are in list/outline form.
    D) mix repetition with variety.

The above quotations (with the exception
of #8) are from Ralph Waldo Emerson's
Representative Men

ANSWERS TO MULTIPLE-CHOICE QUESTIONS

1 - A	4 - C	7 - A	10 - B
2 - B	5 - D	8 - B	
3 - D	6 - D	9 - C	

19
VARIETY
AND
EMPHASIS

KEY TERMS AND CONCEPTS

variety
emphasis
compound sentence
declarative sentence
interrogative sentence
imperative sentence
exclamatory sentence

modifiers
cumulative (loose) sentence
periodic (climactic) sentence
standard word order
inverted word order

FILL-IN QUESTIONS

1. Good writing achieves variety and is less likely
    to be monotonous when its sentence _____   length
    and patterns vary. (19a)

2. Certain ideas can be emphasized by using _____   modifiers
    of different kinds in various positions in the sen-
    tence. (19d)

3. In addition to sounding wordy and childish, strings
    of too many short sentences rarely communicate the
    _____ between major and minor ideas.   relationships
    (19a)

4. However, used sparingly, a short sentence may add
    _____ if used carefully with longer, well-   impact
    crafted sentences. (19a)

5. Writers must be careful not to _____ a sen-   compound
    tence by merely stringing clauses together with "and"
    and "but" while neglecting to think how each idea
    relates to others. (19a)

6. The most common type of English sentence, the   declarative
   _____ sentence, makes a statement and
   can be used in a great variety of sentence
   patterns and structures. (19b)

7. _____ sentences ask questions and may   Interrogative
   help a writer involve the reader, as might also
   a mild command where an _____ sentence   imperative
   urges the reader to consider a point or take
   some action. (19b)

8. Strong commands, as well as _____ sen-   exclamatory
   tences, end with an exclamation point. (19b)

9. The _____ of a sentence establishes the   subject
   focus for that sentence and should be chosen to
   reflect the desired emphasis. (19c)

10. To achieve variety and emphasis, expand basic
    structures with _____ words, phrases   modifying
    and clauses. (19d)

11. Readers are more likely to remember a message at
    the very beginning or the _____ of a sentence.   end
    (19d)

12. The common cumulative or _____ sentence   loose
    adds information by placing modifiers after the
    subject and verb. (19d)

13. The _____ or climactic sentence builds to   periodic
    a climax, saving the main idea for last. (19d)

14. The verb follows the subject in standard word order
    for English sentences, so variations from this set
    pattern, used sparingly, can create effective
    _____. (19e)   emphasis

15. To emphasize their meaning, sometimes good writers
    repeat one carefully chosen word that contains a
    main idea or that uses _____ to focus   rhythm
    on a main idea. (19f)

MULTIPLE-CHOICE QUESTIONS

1. "Thousands of people were watching. Some of the people were   (19a)
   school children. The children wanted to see their teacher.
   Christa McAliffe was from New Hampshire. She was to be the
   first teacher in space." The above group of sentences
   A) demonstrates effective repetition.
   B) avoid monotonous sentence length.
   C) should be revised for variety and emphasis.
   D) establish clear relationships among ideas.

79

2. The sample sentence in question #1 could best be revised   (19a)
   A) by creating a mix of one long and one short sentence.
   B) by adding conjunctions to join the clauses.
   C) shortening clauses to phrases and words.
   D) both (A) and (C)

3. "N.A.S.A. thought about emergency equipment but they thought   (19a)
   it would be too heavy so the officials concluded that shuttle
   mishaps were not survivable and they concentrated on avoiding
   accidents." The above sentence
   A) strings too many compounds together.
   B) establishes a clear focus on the subject of "survival".
   C) moves toward a climax.
   D) all of the above

4. The sample sentence in question #3 could be revised by   (19a)
   A) using participial phrases.
   B) using subordination.
   C) creating adverb clauses.
   D) all of the above

5. "Future emergency provisions would allow crew members to   (19b)
   escape from the shuttle before hitting the water." The
   above sentence is
   A) interrogative.
   B) declarative.
   C) imperative.
   D) exclamatory.

6. The sample sentence in question #5 is also   (19d)
   A) compound.
   B) climactic.
   C) cumulative.
   D) both (A) and (C)

7. "Imagine the horror of falling 65,000 feet into the ocean   (19b)
   and being able to do nothing to prevent it." The above
   sentence
   A) inverts standard word order.
   B) is declarative.
   C) is imperative (in a mild form).
   D) both (A) and (C)

8. "Attached to its boosters, arching high over the Florida   (19d)
   coast, the shuttle burst into flame." The above sentence
   A) is periodic.
   B) is loose.
   C) is cumulative
   D) both (B) and (C)

9. The sample sentence in question #8   (19d)
   A) inverts subject-verb patterns.
   B) follows standard word order.

C) builds to a climax.
D) both (B) and (C)

10. "Not until the Challenger explosion did many Americans   (19e)
    question the space program." The above sentence
    A) uses standard subject-verb pattern.
    B) is interrogative.
    C) gains emphasis by variation.
    D) both (A) and (C)

ANSWERS TO MULTIPLE-CHOICE QUESTIONS

1 - C   4 - D   7 - C   10 - C

2 - D   5 - B   8 - A

3 - A   6 - C   9 - D

20
UNDERSTANDING THE MEANING OF WORDS

KEY TERMS AND CONCEPTS

etymology	general words
pronunciation symbols	specific words
inflected forms	concrete words
usage labels	abstract words
colloquial	prefix
slang	root
unabridged dictionary	suffix
abridged dictionary	context
specialized dictionary	restatement context clue
synonym	contrast context clue
denotation	example context clue
connotation	general sense context clue

FILL-IN QUESTIONS

1. We can learn about the origins and historical development of a word (its changes in form and meaning over the years) by studying its _____ _____. (20a)   etymology

2. A good dictionary gives you not only the spelling, meaning(s) and etymology of a word, but also its phonetic _____, grammatical forms and functions, synonyms and related words as well as its use in the context of a sentence. (20a)   pronunciation

3. The _____ label that a dictionary cites can give you a good idea whether a word is colloquial or slang and, therefore, not appropriate in formal writing. (20a)   usage

4. A good _____ or "shortened" diction-   abridged
   ary is not as in-depth, accurate or complete as one
   like the Oxford English Dictionary, but it contains
   the most commonly used words and can serve the needs
   of most college students. (20a)

5. The explicit dictionary meaning of a word is its
   _____, its definition. (20b)   denotation

6. In contrast, the _____ of a word   connotations
   go beyond the strict definition to convey
   emotional overtones and pleasant or unpleasant
   associations connected with it. (20b)

7. General words relate to an overall group while
   _____ words identify individual   specific
   items in a group. (20b)

8. Abstract words denote qualities, concepts, relationships, acts, conditions or ideas that cannot be
   perceived with the senses while _____   concrete
   words identify what can be seen, heard, tasted, felt
   or smelled. (20b)

9. The _____ is the base or central part   root
   of a word to which prefixes and suffixes are added
   to modify its meaning and grammatical function.
   (20c)

10. You can increase your vocabulary also by learning
    to use _____ clues, the familiar   context
    words that surround an unknown word, which can
    give hints about the new word's meaning. (20c)

MULTIPLE-CHOICE QUESTIONS

1. If I buy a "college" dictionary at a reputable book store,   (20a)
   I can expect it to give me
   A) entries for more than 500,000 English words.
   B) not more than about 200,000 entries.
   C) spelling, pronunciation and synonyms only.
   D) extensive etymology with all obsolete meanings.

Sample Dictionary Entry--

       dough (do) n. 1) a soft, thick mixture of flour or
           meal, liquids and various dry ingredients that
           is baked as a bread, pasty or the like. 2) any
           similar pasty mass. 3) Slang. Money. [Middle
           English dogh, Old English dag]

83

2. In the sample dictionary entry, the information given in (20a)
   parenthesis
   A) probably refers to a key at the bottom of the page.
   B) is the phonetic pronunciation of the word.
   C) is the archaic spelling of the word.
   D) both (A) and (B)

3. In the sample entry, the information given immediately after (20a)
   ' the number three
   A) is the etymology of the word.
   B) is a usage label.
   C) indicates the most recent standard definition.
   D) both (A) and (C)

4. In the sample entry, the underlined letter following the (20a)
   closed parenthesis indicates that
   A) the word derives from the Norse language.
   B) the word is used as a negative.
   C) the word is used as a noun.
   D) both (A) and (C)

5. In the entry the information that follows the number one (20b)
   A) is the denotative meaning of the word.
   B) indicates connotations of the word.
   C) is the chief dictionary definition of the word.
   D) both (A) and (C)

6. A sign on the highway advertises "Pre-owned mobile homes." (20b)
   From the wording, we might conclude that the advertisers
   A) are offering a phony deal.
   B) are avoiding words with negative connotations.
   C) don't know the difference between "trailer" and
      "home."
   D) don't know the difference between "used" and
      "pre-owned."

7. "She fed the children a well-balanced, nutritious meal." (20b)
   The terms in the above sentence are chiefly
   A) general.
   B) specific.
   C) connotative.
   D) concrete.

8. "She fed the children baked chicken, macaroni and cheese, (20b)
   lettuce and tomato salad with carrot sticks, followed by
   oatmeal cookies and a glass of milk." The terms in the
   above sentence are
   A) general.
   B) specific.
   C) abstract.
   D) individual.

9. If we find the word "transposition" in our reading, but do   (20c)
   not quite know its meaning, we could isolate the following
   factor to help us define it:
   A) the Latin root <u>poser</u>, meaning "to place."
   B) the suffix "tion" indicating it is an adjective.
   C) the prefix "trans" meaning "across."
   D) both (A) and (C)

10. Suppose, in our reading, we find the following sentence: (20c)
    "Economists are hoping that new markets abroad will help
    ameliorate depressed economic conditions in the region."
    Even if we are unfamiliar with the term "ameliorate," we
    might guess that it means "to improve" or "to make better"
    from
    A) the general sense context clues.
    B) the use of concrete terms.
    C) analysis of the suffix.
    D) the use of an example.

ANSWERS TO MULTIPLE-CHOICE QUESTIONS

1 - B	4 - C	7 - A	10 - A
2 - D	5 - D	8 - B	
3 - B	6 - B	9 - D	

21
UNDERSTANDING THE EFFECT OF WORDS

KEY TERMS AND CONCEPTS

diction
informal tone
medium-level language
highly formal tone
edited (standard) American English
sexist language
gender specific pronoun
slang
colloquial language
regional (dialectic) language
slanted language
figurative language
simile
metaphor
mixed metaphor

understatement
personification
irony
onomatopoeia
metonymy
synecdoche
oxymoron
cliche
vogue word or phrase
proverb
pretentious language
jargon
euphemism
"doublespeak"
bureaucratic language

FILL-IN QUESTIONS

1. Careful attention to _____ or word choice helps a writer communicate clearly and convincingly. (21a)

   diction

2. Informal language creates an informal _____ (or attitude of the writer toward the subject and audience) and may use slang, colloquialisms, regionalism, sentence fragments and contractions to create the effect of casual speech. (21a)

   tone

3. In contrast, a highly _____ tone or level of language usually uses a polysyllabic Latinate vocabulary

   formal

and often stylistic flourishes and extended figures of speech.   (21a)

4. Neither too casual nor too scholarly, a _____ level language (edited American English) uses standard vocabulary, few contractions, conventional sentence structure, and is acceptable for academic writing intended for general audience. (21a)

medium

5. One of the most widespread occurrence of _____ language is the use of "he" as a generic pronoun referring to someone of unidentified sex, but this problem can be avoided by revising the sentence to a plural.   (21a)

sexist

6. Replacing slang, regional dialect, and _____ language (which are characteristic of casual conversation) with medium level language in writing allows the writer to communicate with a larger group of general readers.   (21a)

colloquial

7. If your language is _____, biased or emotionally loaded, a neutral audience will doubt your ability to think rationally and write fairly about your subject.   (21a)

slanted

8. Using words for more than their literal meaning, _____ language creates comparisons and connections by making one idea or image enhance or explain another.   (21b)

figurative

9. Overused, worn-out expressions, _____ and vogue words are tiresome, trite and have lost their power to communicate effectively.   (21c)

cliches

10. Using _____, or the specialized vocabulary of a particular group, unnecessarily or failing to explain it to an unspecialized audience, creates a showy, pretentious failure of communication.   (21d)

jargon

11. If you attempt to avoid shocking someone or avoid hurting someone's feelings or avoid creating unpleasant pictures by using _____ (pleasant-sounding,"tactful" words in place of "harsh" reality) you can mask the truth and meaning in your writing.   (21d)

euphemisms

12. Similar to euphemism, "_____" attempts to hide reality, but it is a deliberate effort to deceive, distort and confuse its audience.   (21d)

doublespeak

13. Although it is as confusing as "doublespeak," _____ language does not deliberately try

bureaucratic

to mislead, but its carelessly written, stuffy,
ambiguous and wordy language gets in the way of
clear meaning.   (21d)

MULTIPLE-CHOICE QUESTIONS

Selection I

My hound's so good he can sniff a 'coon a mile away and
run like a house 'afire.

1. The diction in Selection I might best be described as   (21a)
    A) illiterate.
    B) colloquial.
    C) medium level.
    D) highly formal.

2. One factor that characterize the level of Selection I   (21a)
    A) misspellings.
    B) fragments.
    C) contractions.
    D) subject matter.

3. The terms "a mile away " and "run like a house 'afire" in
    Selection I might best be described as
    A) slang.
    B) jargon.
    C) cliches.
    D) proverbs.

Selection II

We feel somehow inferior and left out of things by all the marvelous
sensory technology in the creatures around us. We sometimes try to
diminish our sense of loss (or loss of sense) by claiming to ourselves that
we have put such primitive mechanisms behind us in our evolution. We like
to regard the olfactory bulb as a sort of archeological find, and we speak
of the ancient olfactory parts of the brain as though they were elderly,
dotty relatives in need of hobbies.

Lewis Thomas--Lives of a Cell

4. The diction in Selection II might best described as   (21a)
    A) euphemistic.
    B) colloquial.
    C) medium level.
    D) highly formal.

5. In Selection II the comparison of the olfactory parts of   (21b)
    the brain to "elderly, dotty relatives" is an example of
    A) figurative language.
    B) mixed metaphor.

C) a simile.
D) both (A) and (C)

6. The sentences in Selection II (21d)
   A) call attention to themselves with complex structures.
   B) contain slanted, emotionally loaded language.
   C) are conventional in structure.
   D) both (A) and (B)

Selection III

There are men who always confound the praise of goodness with the practice, and who believe themselves mild and moderate, charitable and faithful because they have exerted their eloquence in commendation of mildness, fidelity, and other virtues.

Samuel Johnson--from the Rambler

7. The diction in Selection III might best be described as (21a)
   A) colloquial.
   B) medium level.
   C) highly formal.
   D) bureaucratic language.

Selection IV

By and large, odorants are chemically small, Spartan compounds. In a rose garden, a rose is a rose because of geranoil, a 10-carbon compound, and it is the geometric conformation of atoms and their bond angles that determine the unique fragrance.

Lewis Thomas--The Lives of a Cell
(Essay originally appeared in the New England Journal of Medicine)

8. The diction of Selection IV (21d)
   A) is highly formal.
   B) contains unnecessary jargon.
   C) contains a specialized vocabulary that is appropriate to an audience with some background in chemistry.
   D) contains "doublespeak."

Selection V

Steriods are marvelously odorous, emitting varieties of musky, sexy smells. Women are acutely aware of the odor of a synthetic steroid named exaltolide, which most men are unable to detect.

9. In Selection V, author Lewis Thomas (21a)
   A) uses demeaning and patronizing labels.
   B) revises gender pronouns to the plural.

89

C)   sterotypes roles by gender.
D)   rightly differentiates between male and female abilities.

Selection VI

   I engage in piscatorial activities for the gratifying pleasures they afford but primarily for the opportunities to surround myself with a pulcritudinous environment.

                         (Translation: I fish for the fun of it, but
                         mostly to enjoy the scenery.)

10. The author of the original Selection VI uses   (21d)
     A)   pretentious language.
     B)   figurative language.
     C)   euphemism.
     D)   bureaucratic language.

11. During the Viet Nam War, the term "protective reactive   (21d)
     strike" was used routinely in official reports describing
     American bombing missions. Such a term is probably an
     example of
     A)   "doublespeak."
     B)   deliberate use of irony.
     C)   onomatopoeia.
     D)   a cliche.

ANSWERS TO MULTIPLE-CHOICE QUESTIONS

1 - B   4 - C   7 - C   10 - A

2 - C   5 - D   8 - C   11 - A

3 - C   6 - C   9 - D

22
SPELLING
AND
HYPHENATION

KEY TERMS AND CONCEPTS

proofreading
preferred spelling
mnemonic device
spelling patterns (rules)
homonyms
American spelling
British spelling
variant form
multiple forms
faulty (imprecise) pronunciation

contraction
possessive pronoun
suffix
prefix
open compound
closed compound
hyphenated compound
suspended hyphens

FILL-IN QUESTIONS

1. Two techniques for catching typographical errors
    include reading a page _____ to isolate
    words from the context and using a ruler to focus
    on only _____ line at a time. (22a)

    backward

    one

2. The _____ spelling of a word is usually
    the first one listed on most college dictionaries
    and is the form student writers should select and
    use consistently. (22b)

    preferred

3. A mnemonic device, a technique to improve _____
    _____, can be used to remember a word by
    associating it with a simpler, more familiar word.
    (22b)

    memory

4. Misspelling usually occur in _____, many
    of which correspond to "rules" or descriptive

    patterns

generalizations that can be made to help master the
spelling of several words. (22b)

5. Although they are spelled differently, _____
    _____ are words that sound similar to or exactly   homonyms
    like others, such as "affect" and "effect." (22c)

6. British and American spellings sometimes vary from
    one another, usually in the _____ of   endings
    words; although both spellings are considered
    "correct," in the U.S. students writers should
    use the _____ form consistently   American
    throughout a paper. (22c)

7. Words with _____ forms are words that   multiple
    may be spelled as one word or two, depending on
    meaning, such as "already" and "all ready."
    (22c)

8. Many words, such as "environment," are misspelled
    because of faulty _____. (22c)   pronunciation

9. Some spelling problems are caused when changes
    must be made in the base word before a _____   suffix
    ____ ending can be added to it, as in "advise"
    and "advisable." (22d)

10. When these certain syllables are added in front
    of a base word, _____ either change or   prefixes
    add to the word's meaning and do not change the
    spelling of the base word although a _____   hyphen
    may be required between them. (22d)

11. Single syllable words and very short words should
    never be _____ when they are the last   divided
    word on a line next to the right margin. (22e)

12. If a word must be divided at the end of a line, it
    must be divided between _____, and the   syllables
    writer must never leave or carry over only one or
    two letters. (22e)

13. An open compound word such as "day lily" is written
    as two words; a _____ compound such as   closed
    "homework" is written as one word, but other
    compounds may require a _____ to make   hyphen
    them easier to read, as in post-test. (22e)

1. The word "effect" is a   (22c)
    A) verb that means "to produce an influence on."
    B) noun that means "an emotional response."
    C) noun that means "result."
    D) both (A) and (C)

2. The word "altogether"   (22c)
    A) is a misspelling of "all together."
    B) means "thoroughly."
    C) means "everyone or everything in one place."
    D) means "fully prepared."

3. In Liberia, a brightly decorated public jeepney bus was   (22c)
    spotted with the slogan "Except the Lord!" painted on its
    side. The sign
    A) contained a suffix error.
    B) contained a homonym error.
    C) should have read "accept" instead.
    D) both (B) and (C)

4. "When the state council on public buildings approved   (22c)
    restoration of the capital building, there was no dissent
    from taxpayers." In the above sentence
    A) "council" is misspelled.
    B) "capital" is misspelled.
    C) "dissent" is misspelled.
    D) there is no spelling error.

5. "Once we took off, our ascent was so rapid that I could   (22c)
    hardly bear to breathe, much less to talk." In the above
    sentence
    A) "ascent" is misspelled.
    B) "bear" is misspelled.
    C) "breathe" is misspelled.
    D) there is no error.

6. "When her death was immanent, it was humane to give her   (22c)
    morphine to lessen the pain." In the above sentence
    A) "immanent" should be spelled "imminent."
    B) "immanent" should be spelled "eminent."
    C) "lessen" should be spelled "lesson."
    D) both (A) and (C)

7. "The rider let lose of the rains once she had passed through   (22c)
    the gate; then she rode into the pasture." In the above
    sentence there
    A) is one spelling error.
    B) are two spelling errors.
    C) are three spelling errors.
    D) are not errors in spelling.

8. "Its a test of patience to raise miner children, especially   (22c)
    when their teenagers." In the above sentence there
    A) is one spelling error.
    B) are two spelling errors.
    C) are three spelling errors.
    D) are four spelling errors.

9. "I learned a great deal from Kenneth Clark, who hosted a   (22c)
    fascinating television series entitled Civilization that
    traced connections between ideas and the arts throughout
    history." In the above sentence, written by an American
    in the U.S.,
    A) "connections" is misspelled.
    B) Civilisation is misspelled.
    C) Civilisation is an unacceptable variant in the U.S.
    D) Civilisation is acceptable because it is the title of
        a program series produced in Great Britain.

10. If the sample sentence for question #9 had been written by   (22c)
    by a British student in England,
    A) Civilisation would have been written Civilization.
    B) "learned" would have been spelled "learnt."
    C) probably no spelling changes would have occurred.
    D) both (A) and (B)

11. "We hope that it may be all right to visit you every day."   (22c)
    The above sentence contains
    A) correctly used multiple form expressions.
    B) correctly used open compound words.
    C) an error in the use of "every day."
    D) an error in the use of "all right."

12. "My attempts at basketball were disasterous because I don't   (22c)
    have the strength or heighth to be an athlete of that kind."
    The above sentence contains
    A) one spelling error.
    B) two spelling errors.
    C) three spelling errors.
    D) errors in spelling.

13. "There is never predictable resistance when an immovable   (22c)
    object encounters an irresistable force." In the above
    sentence
    A) "predictable" is misspelled.
    B) "resistance" is misspelled.
    C) "irresistable" is misspelled.
    D) "immovable" is misspelled.

14. "You're confident grasp of the clown role was obvious when   (22d)
    you were dancing comically in front of the crowd." In the
    above sentence which word should be spelled another way?
    A) "you're."
    B) "confident."
    C) "comically."
    D) both (A) and (B)

94

15. "Because several teachers were retiring, we proceded to give   (22d)
    them a retirement party, but weren't permitted to do the same
    for those who were quitting." In the above sentence
    A) "retirement" is misspelled.
    B) "proceded" is misspelled.
    C) "quitting" is misspelled.
    D) no word is misspelled.

16. "Because the niece of the foreign financier had caught the   (22d)
    chief counterfeiter, police were able to seize a freight
    car that yielded weird money hidden in the ceiling." The
    above sentence contains
    A) one spelling error.
    B) two spelling errors.
    C) four spelling errors.
    D) no spelling errors.

17. "One of my heros is the guy who sticks the pimentos in the   (22d)
    olives, but neither of my mothers-in-law would even drink
    martinis." There is a plural form error in
    A) "heros."
    B) "pimentos."
    C) "mothers-in-law."
    D) both (A) and (B)

18. If you were ending a line of an essay with the word   (22e)
    "condominium," the best procedure would be to
    A) write out the whole word, even if filling the margin.
    B) shorten it to "condo" instead.
    C) divide it after "condo-" in this manner.
    D) divide it between any syllable to maintain the margin.

19. Which of the following is the correct plural form of the   (22d)
    word?
    A) data.
    B) condominium.
    D) memorandum.
    D) syllabus.

20. Which of the following is incorrectly hyphenated?   (22e)
    A) anti-inflammatory.
    B) pre-Civil War.
    C) maternity-ward.
    D) short-term investment.

ANSWERS TO MULTIPLE-CHOICE QUESTIONS

1 – C	6 – A	11 – A	16 – D
2 – B	7 – B	12 – B	17 – A
3 – D	8 – C	13 – C	18 – C
4 – B	9 – D	14 – A	19 – A
5 – D	10 – B	15 – B	20 – C

23

THE PERIOD, QUESTION MARK, AND EXCLAMATION POINT

<u>KEY TERMS AND CONCEPTS</u>

end punctuation
abbreviation
acronym
indirect question
direct question

mild command
strong command
emphatic declaration
exclamation point

<u>FILL-IN QUESTIONS</u>

1. The period, question mark and exclamation point are
    called _____ punctuation because of where   end
    they occur in a sentence. (23a)

2. Most abbreviations for states, names of some organ-
    izations and government agencies as well as _____   acronyms
    _____ (initials pronounced as words) do not require
    periods. (23b)

3. An indirect question, which simply reports a question
    rather than asking it, ends with a _____.   period
    (23c)

4. Questions in a series are each followed by a question
    mark, whether or not each question is a _____   complete
    sentence. (23c)

5. Use a question mark in parentheses for a _____   doubtful
    date or number. (23d)

6. If a _____ is phrased as a question, it does   request
    not always require a question mark. (23c)

97

7. Use a question mark after a direct question but do not _____ it with a comma, a period or an exclamation point. (23c)

combine

8. Use an exclamation point to issue a strong _____ _____ or an emphatic declaration. (23e)

command

9. In academic writing, your _____ of words, not exclamation points, better communicates the strength of your message. (23f)

choice

10. If you overuse exclamation points, your reader will think that you _____ the urgency of the point you want to make. (23f)

exaggerate

MULTIPLE-CHOICE QUESTIONS

1. "Edgar Allan Poe lived a short life of poverty, anxiety and tragedy, yet he made significant contributions to American literature." The above sentence is
   A) a statement
   B) a mild command.
   C) an indirect question.
   D) a direct question.

(23a)

2. "Imagine the frantic grief Poe must have felt when he realized his young wife was dying of the same disease that killed his mother." The above sentence is
   A) a statement
   B) a mild command.
   C) an indirect question.
   D) a direct question.

(23a)

3. "At the time, few asked how he could be so productive amid his suffering____" As end punctuation, the above sentence requires
   A) an exclamation point.
   B) a question mark.
   C) a period.
   D) both (B) and (C)

(23a)

4. "Poe's poem 'The Raven,' first written in June, 1844 (?) and published in the _Mirror_, became one of his most popular works." The question mark in the above sentence indicates
   A) a possible error in factual reporting.
   B) the end of a direct question within a statement.
   C) could be replaced with the word "about."
   D) both (A) and (C)

(23d)

5. "Because of his gambling debts, Poe had left the University in Charlottesville, VA, before he could complete a B.A. degree. The abbreviation for Virginia in the above sentence

(23b)

A) has an error in the use of periods.
B) is an acronym.
C) does not require a period.
D) both (B) and (C)

6. "'You must not--you shall not behold this!' said I, shud-   (23e)
dering to [Roderick] Usher, as I led him, with a gentle
violence, from the window." The above sentence from Poe's
"Fall of the House of Usher" contains
A) a strong command giving a firm order.
B) a mild request.
C) an emphatic declaration making a shocking or surprising
        statement.
D) both (B) and (C)

7. The sample sentence in question #6 contains an error   (23e)
A) in use of quotation marks.
B) in commas combined with other punctuation.
C) in use of an exclamation point.
D) none of the above

8. "'And you have not seen it?,' he said abruptly after having   (23c)
stared about him." The above sentence from the same short
story
A) is an indirect question.
B) has an error in punctuation.
C) should end with a question mark.
D) none of the above

9. "'. . . I became aware of a distant, hollow, metalic and   (23f)
clangorous, yet apparently muffled, reverberation.
'. . . Now hear it? Yes, I hear it, and have heard it.
Miserable wretch that I am! I dared not speak! We have put
her living in the tomb!'" The above passage from the short
story
A) lacks punch because it overuses exclamation points.
B) is a suitable example of academic writing.
C) is a dramatically written portrait of hysteria.
D) requires a better choice of words.

10. The words "Now hear it?" in the sample sentence for   (23c)
question #9
A) require a period rather than a question mark.
B) should have an exclamation point for impact.
C) should be omitted because they comprise an incomplete
        sentence.
D) none of the above

ANSWERS TO MULTIPLE-CHOICE QUESTIONS

1 - A	4 - D	7 - D	10 - D
2 - B	5 - C	8 - B	
3 - C	6 - A	9 - C	

24
THE
COMMA

KEY TERMS AND CONCEPTS

coordinating conjunction
independent clause
compound sentence
introductory adverb clause
phrase
introductory phrase or word
transitional expressions
interjections
items in a series
coordinate adjectives

nonrestrictive elements
restrictive elements
appositive
parenthetical expressions
direct address
tag question
explanatory words
speaker tags

FILL-IN QUESTIONS

1. When creating a compound sentence, use a comma
   _____ the coordinating conjunction that   before
   links the independent clauses. (24a)

2. A comma should not be inserted before the conjunction if it only _____ two words, phrases   links
   or dependent clauses. (24a)

3. You should avoid creating a comma _____   splice
   by separating two independent clauses with only a
   comma; follow the comma with a _____ or   conjunction
   use a semi-colon instead. (24a)

4. If words, phrases or clauses precede an independent
   clause, insert a comma to indicate the end of the
   _____ element and the beginning of the   introductory
   independent clause. (24b)

5. Although you must use a comma after an introductory
    adverb clause, an adverb clause that _____
    rather than precedes the independent clause does not
    need to be separated from it by a comma.   (24b)

    follows

6. Additionally, when _____ words (such as
    "for example" or "therefore") come at the beginning
    of the sentence, they should be followed by a comma.
    In fact, transitional and _____ expres-
    sions should be set off with commas also when they
    interrupt or appear at the end of the sentence.
    (24f)

    transitional

    parenthetical

7. Most _____ (such as "Ouch!") stand alone
    and are punctuated with an exclamation point, but
    they should be followed by a comma if they begin a
    sentence.   (24b)

    interjections

8. A _____ is a group of three of more
    words, phrases or clauses that are equivalent in
    grammatical structure and in importance; use commas
    to separate individual items (such as "ham, salad,
    sandwiches and beer").   (24c)

    series

9. Use a comma between _____ adjectives
    (when "and" can be inserted between them or their
    order can be reversed without changing the meaning
    of the sentence); however, omit a comma between the
    final coordinate and the modified noun.   (24d)

    coordinate

10. A _____ modifier provides extra infor-
    mation, but is not essential to understand the
    modified term (or terms); thus, this type of mod-
    ifier should be separated from the rest of the
    sentence by commas.   (24e)

    nonrestrictive

11. In contrast, _____ clauses and phrases
    are essential for understanding the meaning of the
    terms they modify and should not be separated from
    the rest of the sentence.   (24e)

    restrictive

12. An appositive is a word or a group of words that
    _____ the noun or noun phrase that pre-
    cedes it; when it does not restrict meaning, this
    modifier should be set off with commas.   (24e)

    rename

13. Transitional and parenthetical expressions, con-
    trasts, words of direct address and tag questions
    should all be set off from the rest of the sen-
    tence because they _____ it but do not
    change its meaning.   (24f)

    interrupt

14. Commas should set off _____ words from
    short explanations in the same sentence, whether

    quoted

the explanatory words come before, between or after
them.   (24g)

15. Accepted _____ dictates when to use   practice
     commas in dates, names, addresses and numbers.
     (24h)

MULTIPLE-CHOICE QUESTIONS

1. "Successful drug programs catch drug abuse at its earliest   (24a)
    stages and get parents involved." The above sentence
    A) needs a comma to precede the conjunction.
    B) is a compound sentence.
    C) has only one independent clause.
    D) both (A) and (B)

2. "In one district, it was too late to start with eight year   (24a)
    olds so drug educators were sent to kindergartens." The
    above sentence
    A) needs a comma to precede the conjunction.
    B) is a compound sentence.
    C) has only one independent clause.
    D) both (A) and (B)

3. "'Crack,' or smokeable cocaine, has become America's fastest   (24e)
    growing and most dangerous drug." The above sentence contains
    A) a nonrestrictive modifier.
    B) a restrictive modifier.
    C) two independent clauses.
    D) an error in comma use.

4. "When smoked, cocaine reaches the brain in ten seconds which   (24b)
    results in a euphoric high followed by a crushing low." The
    comma after the word "smoked"
    A) may be omitted.
    B) should be deleted.
    C) is required.
    D) is an error in comma use.

5. In the sample sentence in question #4, the word group   (24e)
    following "ten seconds"
    A) is a nonrestrictive clause.
    B) is a nonrestrictive phrase.
    C) should be preceded by a comma.
    D) both (A) and (C)

6. "The cycles of ups and downs reinforce the craving, the   (24a)
    result is a powerful chemical dependency within two weeks."
    The above sentence
    A) is a comma splice.
    B) needs a coordinating conjunction.

C) needs a comma to follow the introductory phrase.
D) both (A) and (B)

7. "If a heroin addict says 'crack' is bad, you know it's bad."   (24b)
The above sentence
A) begins with a transitional expression.
B) has an error in comma use.
C) contains an introductory adverb clause.
D) both (A) and (C)

8. "It is cheap plentiful and intensely addictive, a drug with   (24c)
potential for social disruption and individual tragedy com-
parable only to heroin." The above sentence
A) must have a comma after the first "and."
B) should have a comma after "cheap."
C) has no comma error.
D) should use a semicolon after "addictive."

9. "Outmanned and underfunded police officers point to the   (24e)
abundant supply of cocaine as the root of their problem."
In the above sentence, the expression "outmanned and under-
funded"
A) restricts the meaning of police officers to a special
group.
B) includes all police officers.
C) is a nonrestrictive element.
D) both (B) and (C)

10. "Jack Gillette, a Miami police inspector, claims the U.S.   (24e)
is afraid of offending certain political leaders." The
above sentence
A) uses a nonrestrictive modifier.
B) uses a restrictive modifier.
C) contains an appositive.
D) both (A) and (C)

11. "Gillette claims that the war against 'crack' will not be   (24f)
won by campaigns to reduce public demand, in spite of Reagan
administration optimism, because of the widespread social
acceptance of drugs of all types and because of cocaine's
immensely addictive power." The above sentence
A) contains an appositive.
B) uses a parenthetical expression.
C) has an error in comma use.
D) both (A) and (C)

12. "'On December 7, 1941, the Japanese bombed Pearl Habor, and   (24g)
we went to war,' says Gillette. 'Today, little white packets
are being dropped on this country, and nobody gives a damn,
do they?'" The above sentence contains
A) direct address.
B) explanatory words.
C) a tag question.
D) both (B) and (C)

13. The sample sentence in question #12 has a comma error   (24g)
   A) after an introductory element.
   B) between coordinate adjectives.
   C) after quoted words.
   D) The sentence has no comma errors.

ANSWERS TO THE MULTIPLE-CHOICE QUESTIONS

1 - C	5 - D	8 - B	11 - B
2 - D	6 - D	9 - A	12 - D
3 - A	7 - C	10 - D	13 - D
4 - A			

25
THE
SEMICOLON

independent clause   conjunctive adverb
comma splice   transitional expression
coordinating conjunction   dependent clause

FILL-IN QUESTIONS

1. The semicolon is used most often between closely
    related _____ clauses; it communicates a   independent
    greater separation than a comma would, but less than
    a _____ would suggest. (25a)   period

2. Writers must be careful to avoid using merely a comma
    between independent clauses, which would result in a
    comma _____. (25a)   splice

3. Although independent clauses joined by a coordinating
    conjunction (such as "and" or "but") usually use a
    comma to separate them, a semicolon will add a clearer
    separation when the clauses contain _____   commas
    used in other ways. (25b)

4. When conjunctive _____ (such as "therefore"   adverbs
    or "nevertheless") and other transitional expressions
    join independent clauses, use a semicolon to separate
    them. (25c)

5. You use a semicolon before the expressions mentioned
    in question #4; however, don't forget to use a
    _____ immediately after the expression.   comma
    (25c)

6. If only a comma is used to separate independent clauses joined by a conjunctive adverb or transitional expression, the result will be a comma _____. (25c)   splice

7. When, however, a conjunctive adverb or a transition comes somewhere within the independent clause, and after the first word, set it off with _____. (25c)   commas

8. When your sentence contains a long _____ of words, phrases or clauses that contain commas, use semicolon to separate the items. (25d)   series

9. Avoid making an unclear connection by using a semicolon between a _____ (or subordinate clause) and an independent clause. (25e)   dependent

10. Use a _____ rather than a semicolon to introduce a list. (25e)   colon

MULTIPLE-CHOICE QUESTIONS

1. "Psychologists have tested the ability to predict an individual's personality claimed by many astrologers; such predictions involve 'birth charts' based upon the position of the planets at the time of the person's birth." The above sentence contains   (25a)
   A) a comma splice.
   B) two independent clauses.
   C) a coordinating conjunction.
   D) both (A) and (B)

2. In the sample sentence for question #1, the ideas   (25a)
   A) are not closely related.
   B) should be separated with a period.
   C) are appropriate for separation by a semicolon.
   D) should be separated by a comma.

3. "One test, done ten years ago, required twenty astrologers, who were practicing professionals, to match ten charts with ten case histories; but the individual cases included a musician, a veterinarian, a prostitute, and a librarian." In the above sentence, the semicolon   (25b)
   A) should be omitted.
   B) should be replaced by a comma.
   C) makes the use of commas more clear.
   D) both (A) and (B)

4. "The same task was given to twenty psychologists and social workers, who guessed at chance level, the astrologers did better, with three of them getting all ten correctly matched." The above sentence contains   (25a)

A) a comma splice after "level."
B) a comma splice after "workers."
C) a dependent clause after "level."
D) no error in punctuation.

5. "In another test, four leading astrologers guessed the sun   (25c)
   signs, often linked to appearance, of twelve people after
   a brief interview; in fact, they succeeded with eight of
   the twelve." The semicolon in the above sentence
   A) could correctly be changed to a comma.
   B) could correctly be changed to a period.
   C) requires a coordinating conjunction.
   D) joins a dependent clause to a independent.

6. The sample sentence in question #5   (25c)
   A) begins with a conjunctive adverb.
   B) joins clauses with a transition.
   C) requires the semicolon to come after "in fact."
   D) is a comma splice.

7. "Astrologers point out that even twins are not born at   (25c)
   exactly the same moment, however, they often have very
   similar careers and deaths." The above sentence
   A) contains a comma splice.
   B) requires a semicolon after "moment."
   C) requires a semicolon after "however."
   D) both (A) and (B)

8. The sample sentence in question #7 also should   (25c)
   A) be divided with a period after "however."
   B) eliminate the conjunctive adverb.
   C) should have a comma after "however."
   D) have no additional punctuation.

9. "Identical twins are far more alike in personality and   (25e)
   appearance; although the interval between the births of
   identical and fraternal twins is similar." In the above
   sentence
   A) the comma splice can be eliminated with a period.
   B) the semicolon should be replaced with a comma.
   C) the semicolon should be omitted entirely.
   D) there is no error in punctuation.

10. "Some broader explanation, other than the claims of tradi-   (25d)
    tional astrology, could include the seasons of the year; or
    other rhythms of the solar system that might affect person-
    ality or destiny." The above sentence uses a semicolon
    A) to link two independent clauses.
    B) to clarify items in a series.
    C) incorrectly.
    D) before a conjunctive adverb.

1 – B	4 – A	7 – D	10 – C
2 – C	5 – B	8 – C	
3 – C	6 – B	9 – C	

26
THE
COLON

colon   standard material
independent clause   bibliographical format
summary   salutation
appositive

FILL-IN QUESTIONS

1. The colon points specifically to material that
    _____ it. (26a)   follows

2. When the colon introduces a quotation, it is pre-
    ceded by an _____ clause. (26a)   independent

3. When words introducing a quotation are not an
    independent clause, use a _____   comma
    betweenthe introductory words and the quotation.
    (26a)

4. Use a colon to introduce statements that
    _____, restate or explain what is said   summarize
    in the independent clause that precedes it. (26a)

5. A colon can lead into a final _____,   appositive
    a word or word group that renames or restates a
    noun or pronoun. (26a)

6. Also use a colon to introduce a _____   list
    or a series of items announced by the preceding
    independent clause. (26a)

7. Use a colon after phrases like "the following" or
   "as follows" but _____ after the words   not
   "such as" or "including." (26a)

8. Use a _____ letter to begin a quotation   capital
   introduced by a colon, a lower-case letter for a
   list or other sets of words that are not an independent clause, and _____ for the first   either
   word of an independent clause or a question following a colon. (26a)

9. In punctuating standard material, use a colon to
   separate a _____ from a subtitle, and   title
   (using MLA bibliographical format) to separate the
   city of publication from the _____ of a   publisher
   book. (26b)

10. A colon also separates hours, _____ and   minutes
    seconds as well as chapter and _____ of   verse
    the Bible. (26b)

MULTIPLE-CHOICE QUESTIONS

1. "Perhaps Euripides was thinking of astrology when he said: (26c)
   'Man's most valuable trait is a judicious sense of what not
   to believe.'" In the above sentence, the colon
   A) indicates that something is to follow.
   B) precedes a dependent clause.
   C) follows an independent clause.
   D) both (A) and (C)

2. A comment by T. H. Huxley: 'The greatest tragedy of science   (26b)
   is the slaying of a beautiful hypothesis by an ugly fact,'
   probably applies to astrology too'." In the above sentence
   A) the colon follows an independent clause.
   B) a comma should replace the colon.
   C) a semicolon should replace the colon.
   D) both (A) and (B)

3. "Did Beethoven, who was born in Bonn on December 16, 1770, at   (26b)
   1:30 p.m., arrive with his fate written in the stars?" The
   colon in the above sentence
   A) is a punctuation error.
   B) separates standard material.
   C) separates minutes from seconds.
   D) both (B) and (C)

4. "Although his sun sign was Sagittarius, his ascendant   (26a)
   (Taurus with Uranus) indicates his most memorable quality:
   Musical genius." In the above sentence, the colon
   A) precedes an independent clause.
   B) divides standard material.

C) leads into a final appositive.
D) both (B) and (C)

5. The sample sentence for question #4 contains an error in   (26a)
   A) punctuation.
   B) capitalization.
   C) sentence structure.
   D) none of the above.

6. "A typical dimestore horoscope would list the following   (26a)
   characteristics for Sagittarius: lovable, idealistic,
   optimistic and lucky." In the above sentence, the colon
   A) correctly introduces a list.
   B) should be replaced by a semicolon.
   C) should be replaced by a comma.
   D) should be removed entirely.

7. "However, Beethoven had many problems, such as: blindness,   (26a)
   a difficult and quarrelsome personality and a disordered
   personal life." The colon in the above sentence
   A) correctly introduces a list.
   B) should be replaced by a comma.
   C) should be followed by a capitalized word.
   D) should be removed entirely.

8. "Astrologers would say that more data besides the sun signs   (26c)
   should be considered, including: the ascendant, where the
   planets and moon fall within the twelve houses, and the
   relationship between these planets." The colon in the above
   sentence
   A) separates a dependent clause from an independent one.
   B) separates a dependent clause from a list.
   C) should be omitted.
   D) both (B) and (C)

9. "When we consider the hundreds of variables to be consid-   (26c)
   ered: we see that 'reading' a birth chart is a complicated
   task." The colon in the above sentence
   A) incorrectly introduces a list.
   B) separates a dependent clause from an independent one.
   C) should be changed to a comma.

10. For further information, read this fascinating book: (26b)
    Eysenck, H. J. and D. K. Nias. Astrology: Science or
    Superstition? New York: St. Martin's 1982. The colon in
    the above sentence separate
    A) the year of publication from page numbers.
    B) the city of publication and the publisher.
    C) the title from the subtitle.
    D) both (B) and (C)

ANSWERS TO MULTIPLE-CHOICE QUESTIONS

1 – D	4 – C	7 – D	10 – D
2 – B	5 – B	8 – C	
3 – B	6 – A	9 – D	

27
THE
APOSTROPHE

KEY TERMS AND CONCEPTS

case
possessive case
indefinite pronoun
plural noun
compound word
individual possession
joint or group possession
contraction

FILL-IN QUESTIONS

1. To show ownership, an apostrophe is used to form
   the _____ case of nouns and indefinite   possessive
   pronouns (such as "Nancy's" or "anyone's"). (27a)

2. When nouns and indefinite pronouns do not end in
   "-s," add _____ to show ownership, but   "'s"
   when _____ nouns (such as "actress")   singular
   end in "-s," you must also add the "'s" ending to
   communicate possession ("an actress's cue").
   (27a)

3. However, when a plural noun ends in "-s," use
   only an _____ to communicate pos-   apostrophe
   session ("five actresses' cues"). (27a)

4. In compound words such as "son-in-law," add the
   "-s" to the _____ word (son-in-law's   last
   job"). (27a)

5. When two people each own some individual part of
   something, add "'s" to _____ noun, but   each
   when you want to show joint ownership or group
   possession, add "'s" only to the _____   last
   noun. (27a)

6. The possessive form of personal pronouns (such as
   "his," "its," "yours," and "theirs") should not
   use an _____ to form them. (27b)   apostrophe

7. The possessive pronouns "its" and "whose" are
   often confused with "it's" and "who's," which are
   _____ meaning "it is" and "who is".   contractions
   (27b)

8. Although contractions are common in speech and
   informal writing, they are usually not acceptable
   in _____ writing. (27c)   formal

9. Apostrophes in contractions indicate the _____   omission
   _____ of one or more letters in a word and also
   the first two numerals in a year (such as "the
   summer of '42") in informal writing. (27c)

10. An apostrophe can also be used to form _____   plurals
    of letters, numerals, symbols and words used as
    terms. (27d)

MULTIPLE-CHOICE QUESTIONS

1. "Nearly everyone's heard about one of history's most   (27a)
   interesting prophets, the French physician Nostradamus."
   In the above sentence the word "history's"
   A) is the possessive case of a noun.
   B) is a plural noun.
   C) contains a punctuation error.
   D) is an indefinite pronoun.

2. In the sample sentence for question #1 the term "everyone's" (27c)
   A) is a possessive case indefinite pronoun.
   B) is a contraction.
   C) would be more appropriate for informal writing.
   D) both (B) and (C)

3. "Nostradamus's writings are in cryptic, obscure language and (27a)
   in scrambled historical order." The first term in the above
   sentence
   A) is a plural possessive.
   B) should drop the final "-s" to be correct.
   C) is a singular possessive noun.
   D) both (B) and (C)

115

4. "The prophecies' difficult form may be an effort to avoid   (27a)
    the Sixteenth Century Inquisition's reign of terror." The
    first noun in the above sentence
    A) should add another "-s" to show possession.
    B) needs only the apostrophe to show possession.
    C) is a plural possessive.
    D) both (B) and (C)

5. In the sample sentence in question #4 the term   (27a)
    "Inquisition's"
    A) is a contraction.
    B) contains an apostrophe error.
    C) is a singular possessive noun.
    D) is a plural possessive noun.

6. "Some translators see Napoleon's and Hitler's rise to power   (27a)
    predicted in the writings." The above sentence contains
    compound nouns
    A) showing individual possession.
    B) indicating joint possession.
    C) that should have only the final apostrophe.
    D) both (B) and (C)

7. "Modern critics, whose focus on scientific cause-and-   (27b)
    effect's denies magic and astrology, also sometimes
    forget they're value to the Sixteenth Century." In
    the above sentence the term "whose"
    A) should be spelled "who's."
    B) is a specific possessive pronoun.
    C) is correct as it is written.
    D) both (B) and (C)

8. In the sample sentence for question #7, the term they're"   (27c)
    A) should be spelled "there."
    B) should be spelled "their."
    C) requires the apostrophe to show possession.
    D) is the indefinite pronoun form.

9. In the sample sentence for question #7, the term "cause-and-   (27a)
    effect's"
    A) is a compound possessive noun.
    B) is a plural noun.
    C) contains an error in the use of the apostrophe.
    D) both (B) and (C)

10. "In the 1500's printers often substituted "y's" for "i's"   (27d)
    and "v's" for "u's" etc., so other factors besides it's
    obscurity make interpretation of Nostradamus's work
    difficult." In the above sentence there is an error in the
    use of an apostrophe to form
    A) the plural of letters.
    B) the plural of years.
    C) the possessive of a personal pronoun.
    D) the possessive of a singular noun.

ANSWERS TO MULTIPLE-CHOICE QUESTIONS

1 - A	4 - D	7 - D	10 - C
2 - D	5 - C	8 - B	
3 - C	6 - A	9 - D	

28
QUOTATION MARKS

KEY TERMS AND CONCEPTS

direct quotation
double quotation marks
single quotation marks
displayed quotation
direct discourse
indirect discourse

"short" works
slang
cliche
word used ironically

FILL-IN QUESTIONS

1. A direct quotation is the _____ words copied   exact
   from a print source or transcribed from a nonprint
   source. (28a)

2. A quotation is considered "short" enough to enclose
   within double quotation marks if it can be typed or
   handwritten to occupy no more than _____ lines   four
   on a page. (28a)

3. Longer quotations should be _____ or begun on   displayed
   a new line, with subsequent lines indented (ten
   spaces if typewritten). (28a)

4. For a quotation within a short quotation, use _____   single
   _____ quotation marks around the inside material and
   double marks round the full, quoted passage that contains the second quote within it. (28a)

5. Enclose a quote of _____ lines of poetry or less   three
   within double quotation marks, use appropriate capitalization and a _____ with a space on each side to   slash
   indicate line endings. (28a)

6. Use double quotation marks at the beginning and end of
   a speaker's words in _____ discourse and begin   direct
   a new paragraph each time the speaker changes. (28a)

7. However, do not use quotation marks for _____   indirect
   discourse, which only reports what speakers have said
   instead of exactly quoting them. (28a)

8. Use double quotation marks around the _____ of   titles
   short published works such as short stories, essays,
   articles from periodicals, pamphlets, poems, songs,
   and individual episodes of radio and television series.
   (28b)

9. Sometimes quotation marks are used to enclose words or
   phrases used ironically, technical terms before they
   are _____, translations of words and phrases,   defined
   and words referred to as words. (28c)

10. However, quotation marks are _____ if they   misused
    enclose inappropriate expressions such as slang and
    cliches in formal writing or if they are used simply to
    call attention to a word. (28d)

11. When using quotation marks with other punctuation,
    place commas and periods _____ closing quo-   inside
    tation marks, put colons and semicolons outside,
    but put question marks, exclamation points and dashes
    inside or outside, according to the context. (28e)

MULTIPLE-CHOICE QUESTIONS

Selection I--
        Late one "sleepless " night, in Act III of Shakespeare's Henry
IV, Part II, King Henry, who had illegally wrested the throne away
from his weak, self-indulgent cousin Richard II, comments to himself
on the burdens of being king:

              Canst thou, O partial Sleep, give thy repose
              To the wet sea boy in an hour so rude,
              And in the calmest and most stillest night,
              With all appliances and means to boot,
              Deny it to a king? Then happy low, lie down!
              Uneasy lies the head that wears a crown.

King Henry, addressing a personified figure of Sleep, had referred
earlier to a young sailor who fell asleep on watch in spite of the
rough seas: "Wilt thou upon the high and giddy mast / Seal up the
ship boy's eyes and rock his brain / In cradle of the rude imperious
surge . . . ."

1. In Selection I, the passage that begins <u>Canst thou</u> is a   (28a)
   direct quote that
   A) should be inclosed within double quotation marks.
   B) is displayed and requires no quotation marks.
   C) should be typed to match normal margin spacing.
   D) is displayed but requires single quotation marks.

2. In Selection I, the passage that begins <u>Wilt thou</u>   (28a)
   A) requires single rather than double quotation marks.
   B) contains errors in capitalization.
   C) uses slashes to indicate line ends.
   D) both (B) and (C)

3. In Selection I, the term <u>Act III</u>   (28b)
   A) should be enclosed by quotation marks.
   B) is the title of a short work contained within a longer one.
   C) is correct as it is punctuated in the passage.
   D) both (A) and (B)

4. In Selection I, the term <u>sleepless</u>   (28c)
   A) is obviously used ironically.
   B) is a direct quote from the passage below it.
   C) is correctly enclosed within double quotation marks.
   D) does not require the quotation marks enclosing it.

5. In Selection I, the punctuation that comes after the word   (28e)
   <u>rude imperious surge</u>
   A) should change to a semicolon outside the quotation mark.
   B) follows accepted practice for punctuation.
   C) combines an ellipsis and a period. (see 29d)
   D) both (B) and (C)

Selection II

    "There is, I believe, in every disposition a tendency to do some particular evil--a natural defect, which not even the best education can overcome."
    "And <u>your</u> defect is a propensity to hate everybody."
    "And <u>yours</u>," he replied with a smile, "is willingness to misunderstand them."
    "Do let us have a little music," cried Miss Bingley, tired of a conversation in which she had no share. "Louisa, you will not mind my waking Mr. Hurst?"

        Jane Austin--<u>Pride and Prejudice</u>

6. The indented lines in Selection II   (28a)
   A) indicate that the passage is displayed.
   B) indicate changes of speakers.
   C) show that the entire passage is a direct quote.
   D) should be uniform with standard margins.

7. From the punctuation in the third sentence in Selection II,   (28a)
   which begins "And yours," he replied, we see that it contains
   A) direct discourse.
   B) indirect discourse.
   C) an interrupted quotation.
   D) both (A) and (C)

8. The question mark that is the end punctuation for Selection   (28e)
   II
   A) should come outside the quotation marks.
   B) should be a period instead.
   C) indicates that there is a quote within a quote.
   D) is appropriately placed for the context.

Selection III

        While they watched "Hill Street Blues," I read "The Blue Hotel,"
   a story by Stephen Crane, in my "Literature" book. Later, my brother
   said that it had been a very good show that night."

9. In Selection III, a correct use of quotation marks is demon-   (28b)
   strated by
   A) "Hill Street Blues."
   B) "The Blue Hotel."
   C) my "Literature" book.
   D) both (A) and (B)

10. The second sentence in Selection III   (28a)
    A) contains direct discourse.
    B) contains indirect discourse.
    C) requires single quotation marks around good show.
    D) requires double quotation marks around it had been a very
        good show that night.

ANSWERS TO MULTIPLE-CHOICE QUESTIONS

1 - B   4 - D   7 - D   10 - B

2 - C   5 - D   8 - D

3 - C   6 - B   9 - B

29
OTHER
MARKS
OF
PUNCTUATION

KEY TERMS AND CONCEPTS

dash (typed)   brackets
"asides"   ellipsis
appositive   parenthetical documentation
parenthesis   broken-off speech
de-emphasize   slash
interrupting material   numerical fractions

FILL-IN QUESTIONS

1. You can use a dash (or dashes) to add information
    that _____ the structure of your   interrupts
    sentence. (29a)

2. The dashes _____ the added material,   emphasize
    whether it is explanation, example, definition or
    even a _____ comment or reaction.   personal
    (29a)

3. When you are typing a sentence and need to make a
    dash, hit the hyphen key twice, but do not leave a
    _____ before, between or after the   space
    hyphens. (29a)

4. When using a dash to emphasize explanations,
    including appositives, examples, and definitions,
    avoid distracting or confusing your _____   reader
    _____; place the words you set off with dashes
    near to or next to the words they _____.   explain
    (29a)

5. If the words you are emphasizing with dashes would require a question mark or exclamation mark if written as a separate sentence, then insert that same punctuation just _____ the second dash. (29a)

before

6. In contrast to dashes, parentheses (which also let you interrupt your sentence to add information) _____ the added material rather than stress it. (29b)

de-emphasize

7. In addition to enclosing interrupting explanations, examples and asides, parentheses are used to enclose certain numbers or letters of _____ items as well as doubtful dates or numbers. (29b)

listed

8. If words coming before parenthetical material require a comma at the end, place the comma immediately _____ the interrupted material and closing parenthesis. (29b)

after

9. When you quote material that needs changes to make it fit your sentence structure, or that needs explanation or clarification, use _____ _____ to enclose the added material. (29c)

brackets

10. Use either a dash or an _____ to indicate hesitant or broken off speech. (29d)

ellipsis

11. Use ellipses to indicate points where you have _____ words from the material you are quoted. (29d)

omitted

MULTIPLE-CHOICE QUESTIONS

Selection I

According to legend, a man who was not chief, but who was deeply respected for his athletic prowess, his skill as a hunter and his intelligence, stood quietly by. He was Osceola, son of a white father [sic] and a Creek mother. . . . On this day, he waited as the American officers attempted to bully the [Seminole] chiefs into signing away their Florida land. . . . At last his name was called. He stepped lightly to the table and, with a sweeping motion, drew his knife and stabbed down savagely on the treaty. "This is the only way I sign!" he cried. Chiefs and officers alike waited in stunned silence.

Virginia Bergman Peters--The Florida Wars

1. In Selection I the use of [sic] in the second sentence   (29c)
   A) means "its is thus in the original."
   B) shows that Osceola was legally a half-breed.

C) indicates a mistake in the quoted material.
D) both (A) and (C)

2. In Selection I, the ellipses after the words "mother" and (29d)
   "land" indicate that material has been
   A) added and emphasized.
   B) added and minimized.
   C) omitted from the quoted passage.
   D) clarified by added information.

3. In Selection I the term [Seminole] is enclosed in brackets (29c)
   to show that it
   A) is not an appropriate term.
   B) did not appear in the original source.
   C) should be emphasized.
   D) is an "aside" or personal view of the author.

4. In Selection I the formation of the ellipses marks (29d)
   A) requires three not four periods.
   B) should leave no extra space between each period.
   C) indicates the end of the sentence.
   D) do not need to be repeated more than once within the
      same quoted passage.

5. "The Mikasuki called Ote-mathla (also known as Jumper) was (29b)
   described as fierce and crafty-looking, but Osceola was
   apparently slight, graceful and handsome." In the above
   sentence, the added material within parentheses
   A) is emphasized.
   B) is not stressed.
   C) is directly quoted.
   D) both (A) and (C)

6. "These two men--Osceola and Jumper--led the resistance that (29a)
   became the Second Seminole War." In the above sentence, the
   dashes enclose material that adds
   A) an appositive.
   B) an example.
   C) a definition.
   D) an "aside."

7. "Just before Osceola's attack, Major Dade turned to his men (29a)
   and said, "We have got through all danger now--keep up good
   heart." In the above sentence, the dash
   A) adds explanatory material.
   B) indicated hesitating or broken off speech.
   C) emphasizes a contrast.
   D) emphasizes an "aside."

8. "General Hernandez, on orders from General Jesup, captured (29a)
   Coacoochee (or Wild Cat) and later Osceola--under a white
   flag of truce!--to break the back of the resistance." In
   the above sentence, the exclamation point should
   A) be moved to the end of the sentence.
   B) be moved outside of the second dash.

124

C) remain where it is.
D) be removed altogether.

9. From the punctuation marks on the sentence for question #8,   (29a)
we can see that the writer
   A) indicates hesitating or broken off speech.
   B) is emphasizing a contrast.
   C) adds an example.
   D) interjects information and expresses a personal
   reaction to it.

10. "After he escaped from the fort prison at St. Augustine   (29b)
(with the help of a Negro chief named John Cavallo) Wild Cat
slipped quietly into the swamps." The above sentence
requires a comma after
   A) "St. Augustine."
   B) the opening parenthesis.
   C) "Cavallo."
   D) the closing parenthesis.

11. "Even military officers at Fort Moultrie grieved Osceola's   (29b)
death in prison because he had demonstrated these qualities:
1 genius in organizing military attacks, 2 a heart bold
enough to lead his chosen people, and 3 dignity and courage
in facing his death." In the above sentence, the numbers of
the listed items should be
   A) set off with semicolons.
   B) set off with a closing parenthesis after each number.
   C) enclosed within parentheses.
   D) set off with a dash.

ANSWERS TO MULTIPLE-CHOICE QUESTIONS

1 - D	4 - C	7 - B	10 - D
2 - C	5 - B	8 - C	11 - C
3 - B	6 - A	9 - D	

30
CAPITALS, ITALICS, ABBREVIATIONS, AND NUMBERS

KEY TERMS AND CONCEPTS

mechanics
capital
lower-case
parenthetical sentences
run-in list
displayed list
introduced quotation
proper noun
common noun
"common" meaning

specific name
brand name
general name
model name
roman type
italic type
underlining
abbreviation
standard practice
spelled-out numbers

FILL-IN QUESTIONS

1. The _____ word in a sentence, question or command should always be capitalized. (30a)

   first

2. If a _____ sentence stands alone, rather than falling within the structure of another sentence, it should start with a capital letter. (30a)

   parenthetical

3. Items in a _____ list are worked into sentence or paragraph structure,; when the items are _____ sentences in themselves, the first word of each should be capitalized. (30b)

   run-in

   complete

4. If an introduced quotation is part of the structure of your own sentence, the first word in the quoted material _____ need to be capitalized. (30c)

   does not

5. Capitalize the interjection "O" and the pronoun "I" but not "_____" unless it begins a sentence or is capitalized in quoted poetry. (30d)   oh

6. _____ adjectives are formed from nouns that name specific persons, places or things, e.g. "Shakespearian" actor. (30e)   Proper

7. Common nouns, which name _____ classes of persons, places or things, should not be capitalized unless they begin a sentence. (30e)   general

8. Titles of long written works, names of ships and some aircraft, titles of films, television series, works of graphic art and sculpture, as well as titles of long musical works, should be _____. (30f)   underlined

9. Underlining, which stands for _____ in typewritten or handwritten manuscripts, also calls attention to words in a foreign language, letters, numbers and words used as terms. (30f)   italics

10. When underlining is used for _____, to clarify a meaning or stress a point, it should be used sparingly to avoid making the writing seem immature. (30g)   emphasis

11. When using a long name or term frequently in a paper, if you spell out the full term on first use (followed by its _____ form in parentheses) you may use the shortened form throughout the rest of the paper. (30h)   abbreviated

12. In general, you must spell out combinations of cities and states, but may use the _____ abbreviation for the state name if you include a full address (street, city and state) within the body of the paper. (30h)   postal

13. Abbreviation in documentation, as well as in figures and spelled-out numbers, should be used according to _____ practice. (30j)   standard

MULTIPLE-CHOICE QUESTIONS

1. "The Nez Perce called themselves Numipu, which meant 'We People,' although the french name was given them for their former custom of wearing a shell in the septum of the nose." In the above sentence the term "Nez Perce" is capitalized because it   (30e)
    A) is a proper adjective.
    B) is a proper noun.

127

C) is a general term.

D) contains an error.

2. In the sample sentence for question #1, the term "french"   (30e)
is not capitalized because it
A) has taken on a common meaning.
B) is not a brand name.
C) is a general term.
D) contains an error.

3. In the sample sentence for question #1, the term <u>Numipu</u> is   (30f)
underlined because it
A) is the title of a long work.
B) stresses a contrast.
C) indicates that the word is from a foreign language.
D) gives the word more emphasis.

4. "Nez Perce Chiefs refused to attack whites, and Lieutenant   (30e)
Lawrence Kipp refers to them as 'Some of the friendly
indians' in his report." In the above sentence both "Chiefs"
and "Lieutenant" are titles, but
A) the first term contains an error.
B) the second term contains an error.
C) the second refers to a specific person.
D) both (A) and (C)

5. In the sample sentence for question #4, both the terms   (30e)
"whites" and "indians" refer to groups of humankind, but
A) the first term contains an error.
B) the second term contains an error.
C) neither refers to a special group.
D) both (B) and (C)

6. In the sample sentence for question #4, the term "Some" is   (30c)
capitalized because it
A) is an introduced quotation.
B) is part of the structure of the author's sentence.
C) directly quotes speech.
D) contains an error.

7. "The greatest and wisest of the Nez Perce leaders, Chief   (30c)
Joseph must also have had a sense of humor, as we can see in
this comment: "When you can get the last word with an echo,
you may have the last word with your wife." In the above
sentence, "When" is capitalized because it
A) begins a sentence.
B) is part of the structure of the author's sentence.
C) begins a run-in list.
D) contains an error.

8. "By 1873, when he was 32 years old, Chief Joseph stood six   (30j)
feet two inches, weighed well over two hundred pounds and
had married four wives." In the above sentence, according
to standard practice for writing in the humanities,
A) "1873" should be spelled out.

B)   "32" should be spelled out.

C)   "six feet two inches" should be written in figures.

D)   "pounds" should be abbreviated.

9.   "That Joseph was not ordinarily a war chief is indicated by   (30f)
     Yellow Wolf, a scout and warrior, in his account His Own
     Story (recorded by L. V. McWhorter) and also in an interview
     with Josiah Red Wolf in the 'Inland Empire Magazine' dated
     Nov. 17, 1963." In the above sentence the underlining of
     the term His Own Story indicates that
     A)   it is the title of a long work.
     B)   it refers to a special group.
     C)   the terms are translated from a foreign language.
     D)   the terms require special emphasis.

10. In the sample sentence for question #9, there is a mechanics   (30f)
     error in
     A)   Nov. 17, 1963.
     B)   L. V. McWhorter.
     C)   'Inland Empire Magazine.'
     D)   both (A) and (C)

11. In the sample sentence for question #9, the word "recorded"   (30a)
     A)   should be capitalized.
     B)   begins a parenthetical sentence.
     C)   is correct as written.
     B)   both (A) and (B)

12. "General O.O. Howard hoped to head them off near Yellowstone   (30e)
     park, but undaunted by the Gatling guns and howitzers, the
     braves shouted taunts at the soldiers." In the above
     sentence there is a mechanics error in
     A)   General O.O. Howard.
     B)   Yellowstone park.
     C)   Gatling guns.
     D)   both (A) and (B)

13. In the sample sentence for question #12, the term "Gatling"   (30e)
     in "Gatling guns" involves
     A)   a general term.
     B)   a common noun.
     C)   a proper adjective.
     D)   a proper noun.

14. "The Nez Perce attempted to pass through the country peace-   (30g)
     ably, buying supplies from Montana settlements, paying for
     them with coins and currency." In the above sentence
     A)   "buying" is meant to be emphasized.
     B)   "settlements" should be capitalized.
     C)   underlining is used to indicate roman type.
     D)   "Montana" can be abbreviated.

15. "After thirty three years of diplomacy and peace efforts,   (30h)
     his people finally exhausted and starving, Chief Joseph
     surrendered one freezing Winter day and left forever his

his beloved Wallowa Valley." In the above sentence there is
a mechanics error in
A) Winter.
B) Wallowa Valley
C) thirty three.
D) both (A) and (C)

ANSWERS TO MULTIPLE-CHOICE QUESTIONS

1 – B	5 – B	9 – A	13 – C
2 – D	6 – D	10 – D	14 – A
3 – C	7 – A	11 – C	15 – D
4 – D	8 – B	12 – B	

31
PARAPHRASING, SUMMARIZING, QUOTING

KEY TERMS AND CONCEPTS

plagiarism
common knowledge
personal knowledge
documentation
paraphrase
acceptable paraphrase
literal level
inferential level
synonyms
summary
transitional expression
formal summary

informal summary
unacceptable summary
acceptable summary
quotation
accepted authority
disembodied quotation

FILL-IN QUESTIONS

1. Presenting another person's words or ideas as your
   own, an act of _____, is a serious   plagiarism
   offense whether it is done deliberately or
   unintentionally.   (31a)

2. Writers are not expected to document what is
   _____ knowledge or their own personal   common
   knowledge.   (31a)

3. However, writers are expected to document the
   source of any material that they directly
   _____, paraphrase or summarize. (31a)   quote

4. If you are writing a research paper, a consistent
   _____ system can help you keep separate   note taking
   and clearly identified all directly quoted material,

summarized or paraphrased material, and your own
thoughts about the material. (31a)

5. To avoid wasting time, frantic last-minute
    searches, and a greater risk of plagiarism,
    collect _____ of your sources as you   documentation
    take notes from the sources. (31a)

6. Documentation is _____ your sources   acknowledging
    by giving full and accurate information about the
    author, title, date of publication and other
    related facts. (31b)

7. Your _____, your detailed restatement   paraphrase
    of someone else's words in your own words, forces
    you to read closely and to extract precise meaning
    from the material you are reading. (31b)

8. Your paraphrase should rephrase the material--not
    quote it, not summarize it, not skip over parts of
    it, and not distort its meaning; the paraphrase
    should also not contain your own _____   thoughts
    and comments, which you will need later to introduce
    and interpret the paraphrased material in the body
    of your paper. (31c)

9. Although your paraphrase reproduces the order of
    ideas and emphasis in the source, it should use your
    own words and phrasing, _____ and your   synonyms
    own sentence structure rather than duplicating
    that of the source. (31c)

10. In contrast to your paraphrase, your _____   summary
    _____ condenses the essentials of someone else's
    thoughts into a few general statements written in
    your own words. (31d)

11. The length of the summary must be in proportion to
    the length of the source you are summarizing,
    usually one _____ per paragraph unless   sentence
    the material is particularly complex. (31d)

12. In a _____ summary, each sentence (in   formal
    which you have summed up the main point of a section
    of the original) must be clearly connected to your
    other summary sentences by appropriate transitions.
    (31d)

14. Quotations should be used as _____ for   support
    your own main points, not substituted for them.
    (31e)

15. Use accurately quoted, relevant material from
    accepted authorities when their language is
    especially striking, when the thought would be

very difficult to _____ accurately,   rephrase
when it is especially important for your thesis,
or when it could be open to alternate _____   interpretation
_____. (31e)

MULTIPLE-CHOICE QUESTIONS

Original I

In the phase of incipient population decline, the conditions for advancement alter significantly. The inner-directed person is able to see industrial and commercial possibilities and to work with the zeal and ruthlessness required by expanding frontiers in the phase of transitional growth of population. Societies in the phase of incipient population decline, on the other hand, need neither such zeal nor such independence. Business, government, the professions, become heavily bureaucratized, as we see most strikingly, for instance, in France. Such societies increasingly turn to the remaining refractory components of the industrial process: the men who run the machines. Social mobility under these conditions continues to exist. But it depends less on what one is and what one does than on what others think of one--and how competent one is in manipulating others and being oneself manipulated. . . .

David Riesman--The Lonely Crowd

Sample I

As the number of people in a society decreases and as it becomes increasingly more industrialized, the productivity and internal character values of individuals become less important than their ability to interact with and manage or use and be used by other people in a newly bureaucratic social environment.

1. Sample I could best be described as an   (31d)
   A) unacceptable paraphrase of the first part of Original I.
   B) acceptable paraphrase of the first part of Original I.
   C) unacceptable summary of Original I.
   D) acceptable summary of Original I.

Sample II

When a society decreases in numbers of people, a change takes place in the rules that govern their chance at upward mobility. At first "inner-directed" (operating from an internalized set of values) individuals struggle to realize the financial goals that open horizons have suggested to them. But when there are fewer people, there is less room for such rugged individualism.

2. Sample II could best be described as an   (31c)
   A) unacceptable paraphrase of the first part of Original I.
   B) acceptable paraphrase of the first part of Original I.

C) unacceptable summary of Original I.
D) acceptable summary of Original I.

Sample III

In times of population decline, conditions for advancement change.
The inner-directed person can see financial possibilities and works hard,
with the necessary zeal and ruthlessness demanded by expanding horizons in
the transitional phase. In the next phase, the population has declined and
society doesn't need these qualities.

3. Sample III could best be described as an   (31c)
   A) unacceptable paraphrase of the first part of Original I.
   B) acceptable paraphrase of the first part of Original I.
   C) unacceptable summary of Original I.
   D) acceptable summary of Original I.

4. Because Reisman first originated the concept of "inner-   (31c)
   directed" individuals
   A) Sample I rightly avoids using the term.
   B) Sample II rightly uses the term.
   C) Sample III rightly uses the term.
   D) The term cannot be used in paraphrase or summary.

5. The first sentence in both Sample II and Sample III suggest   (31c)
   the same idea, but the word choice
   A) in III is too similar to Original I.
   B) in II is too similar to Original I.
   C) in II is better because it is more concise.
   D) in III is better because it is more concise.

6. The sentence structure of Original I is   (31c)
   A) too complex to paraphrase completely.
   B) most closely echoed in Sample I.
   C) most closely echoed in Sample II.
   D) most closely echoed in Sample III.

Original II

"Over the carnage rose prophetic a voice," wrote Walt Whitman,
catching the spirit of that great moment. "Affection shall solve the
problems of freedom yet." Could his prophecy have been fulfilled . . . ?
It certainly might have been, had things been left to the fighting officers
and men. Commissioners appointed by Lee and Grant to arrange practical
details of the surrender had no difficulty reaching an agreement. Grant
not only rushed rations to the half-starved Confederates but allowed them
free transportation home on government ships and railways. As General
Gordon, one of the commissioners, said, courtesy and even deference was
shown to the defeated officers; everyone looked forward to "a liberal,
generous, magnanimous policy" toward the South. A Confederate cannoneer,
who had expected to be "paraded through Northern cities for the benefit of

134

jeering crowds" (as had been done to Union prisoners in Richmond), was relieved to learn that he could go home. There was good-humored chaffing between officers of both sides. General Meade, who had superbly commanded the Army of the Potomac through this last campaign, rode out to meet the Confederate commander, doffed his cap (the old-fashioned army salute), and said, "Good morning, General." Lee remarked, "What are you doing with all that gray in your beard?" To which Meade replied, "You have to answer for most of it!"

Samuel Eliot Morison--The Oxford History of the
American People.

Sample IV

Whitman's prophecy--"Affection shall solve the problems of freedom." --might have been fulfilled, had things been left to the fighting officers and men. There had been no difficulty in reaching agreement about the practical details of the surrender. Courtesy and deference were shown to the defeated officers. Food was rushed to the half-starved soldiers and they were sent home for free on government ships and railways. One such Confederate soldier was relieved to learn that he could go home when he had expected to be paraded through Northern cities for the benefit of jeering crowds.

7. The use that Sample IV makes of Original II can be   (31a)
    considered
    A) clearly plagiarism.
    B) an acceptable summary of it.
    C) an acceptable paraphrase of it.
    D) to need no documentation since the facts are general
        knowledge.

Sample V

When Whitman wrote "Affection shall solve the problems of freedom yet," he caught the spirit of the moment. There had been no difficulties in reaching a surrender agreement and the Confederates had been treated with courtesy and deference. And, as Samuel Eliot Morison points out, if solving the problem of freedom had been left up to the fighting officers and men, there would have been no problem with the rebels returning to the Union. (Morison 700) For example, food was rushed to the half-starved Confederates and they were allowed free transportation home on government ships and railways.

8. The use that Sample IV makes of Original II can be   (31a)
    considered
    A) adequately documented.
    B) plagiarism of facts.
    C) plagiarism of phrasing and wording.
    D) adequate interweaving of writer's own words with source.

Sample VI

The future of the South at the end of the Civil War was at a turning point. Lincoln had promised a conciliatory attitude in his famous "bind up the nation's wounds" speech. Grant's gentlemanly acts of respect and compassion to Lee and his army at Appomatox are also legend. But would such feelings overcome the bitterness on both sides at the horrible losses they had suffered. Apparently it could have ". . . had things been left to the fighting officers and men." (Morison 700) Morison gives several examples of the generosity, compassion and even "good humored chaffing" between the two sides. (700)

9. The use that Sample VI makes of Original II can be considered   (31a)
   A) adequately documented.
   B) plagiarism of facts.
   C) plagiarism of phrasing and wording.
   D) an acceptable paraphrase of it.

10. In Sample VI, the quote by Lincoln   (31a)
   A) also needs documentation of source.
   B) is common knowledge, but needs the attribution.
   C) is personal knowledge.
   D) should have been paraphrased instead of quoted.

ANSWERS TO MULTIPLE-CHOICE QUESTIONS

1 - D	4 - B	7 - A	10 - B
2 - B	5 - A	8 - C	
3 - A	6 - D	9 - A	

32
WRITING
RESEARCH

KEY TERMS AND CONCEPTS

research
primary research
primary source
secondary source
research writing process
research process
headings
key words (descriptors)
documentation style
footnotes (endnotes)
parenthetical references
Modern Language Association
American Psychological Association
search strategy
bibliography
index to periodicals
general index
specialized index
card catalog
call number

Library of Congress System
Dewey Decimal System
tracer
computerized database
abstract
research log
plagiarism
working bibliography
Works Cited list
preliminary thesis statement
revised thesis statement
informal outline
topic outline
sentence outline
first draft
subsequent drafts
final draft

FILL-IN QUESTIONS

1. Some research paper assignments may require you to
   do _____ research, that is to conduct   primary
   experiments and make direct observations, while
   other assignments require you to examine and draw
   from secondary sources, which talk about someone
   else's original work. (32)

2. Although its writing process is similar to all academic writing, the research paper also involves finding, evaluating and _____ information sources into the paper by means of paraphrasing, summarizing and quoting. (31a)

integrating

3. A topic is sufficiently _____ when it fits the assigned length and time period, and when it is specific enough to allow adequate development of the general points with specific details. (32b)

narrow

4. A paper is worth researching when it allows you to draw from a _____ of sources, when it is worth time and attention from you and your reader, and when it is complex enough to stimulate your critical thinking. (32b)

variety

5. When you evaluate you sources, check to see that they have authority, reliability, good support, current information and a _____ tone. (32d)

balanced

6. Researchers use headings (or subject categories in collections of books and periodicals) as well as _____ words or descriptors (which identify subject categories in indexes of periodicals and in computerized databases). You need to find out which headings and words will help you _____ the information you are seeking for your paper. (32d)

key

locate

7. The current Modern Language Association documentation style calls for _____ references in the text of the paper and a Works Cited list of sources at the end instead of footnotes (or endnotes) and a bibliography. (32d)

parenthetical

8. Using a _____ strategy to review the possibilities of interviewing experts, mailing letters, asking for information, and using library resources, you can move from general to specific sources in an organized, efficient and thorough manner. (32e)

search

9. To prepare a good undergraduate research paper, an expert librarian at New York City Library estimates that you will want to examine at least twenty-five different sources and spend at least _____ hours in the library. (32e)

fifteen

10. Annotated or critical bibliographies (which can give especially helpful information about sources) and _____ bibliographies (which list

specialized

many books in a particular subject area) can help
you look for the increasingly specific and focused
information you need in working on your research
paper.   (32e)

11. Both general and specialized indexes to _____   periodicals
     _____ (magazines and journals published at set
     periods during the year) list articles by subject
     and some include a brief abstract or summary of
     the article.   (32e)

12. Whether using either the Library of Congress or the
     Dewey Decimal classification system, a library's
     card catalog can give you the _____   call
     number of a book that tells where it is located in
     the stacks, in addition to tracers that give other
     related _____ which can lead you to   headings
     additional sources.   (32e)

13. A research _____ is a history of your   log
     search strategy and can help you keep track of
     your ideas as you gather information, organize it
     and write your paper.   (32f)

14. When taking notes from your sources, you must first
     decide whether the source is good enough, and then
     decide what to select, trying to keep a _____   balance
     _____ between major and minor information, and
     finally decide how to write the notes so they help
     you avoid the possibility of _____, or   plagiarism
     passing off someone else's words as your own.   (32f)

15. Writing your notes on index cards rather than in a
     notebook can give you greater _____ when   flexibility
     you organize and write your paper; however, never put
     notes from more than one source on the same card, but
     always _____ the source and indicate the   identify
     type of note (whether paraphrase, summary or direct
     quote).   (32f)

16. Following the pattern of examples in your handbook,
     keep track of all your sources by developing a
     _____ bibliography on cards that include   working
     all data necessary for your documentation style; if
     you are using MLA style, you can later use the cards
     to create a _____ list of all the sources   Works Cited
     you actually refer to on the paper.   (32g)

17. Drafting a preliminary _____ statement   thesis
     provides a useful focus on the topic during the
     research process, but the statement may be revised
     during the organizing and writing process to better
     express the central _____ and purpose as   theme
     well as unify the paper and identify its audience.
     (32h)

18. When you try to structure your notes into a unified whole by writing a _____ draft, you may you may gain insights and see new connections in your material. (32j)

    rough

19. Set your rough draft aside for awhile, and then reread and _____, making sure that the ideas are relevant, complete, and adequately developed, that they flow smoothly from one to another without gaps, that they fulfill the promise of the thesis statement, and that they integrate source material without plagiarizing. (32j)

    revise

20. When drafting your paper, insert the appropriate parenthetical _____ to signal points in your paper where you have paraphrased, summarized or quoted from another source, to indicate where that source material is located, and to give information that enables a reader to find the source in your Work Cited. (32k)

    references

33
OBSERVING
A STUDENT
WRITING
RESEARCH

KEY TERMS AND CONCEPTS   (omitted)

FILL-IN QUESTIONS   (reference to Handbook sections omitted)

1. Amy Brown further _____ the topic of   narrowed
    her research paper from "body language" to
    "personal space" when she remembered a personal
    experience.

2. Assuming that her readers would have little expert
    knowledge about her topic, she chose to write for a
    _____ audience.   general

3. Because of the research assignment's length and
    time limit, Brown decided to change the _____   purpose
    _____ of her paper from a persuasive one to an
    informative one.

4. At the beginning of her search strategy, Brown
    read a book recommended by her professor to get a
    broad _____ of her topic.   overview

5. Using key words, Brown checked a specialized index,
    the card catalog, the bibliography at the back of
    one book, and a computerized databased system to
    find the sources that made up her working
    _____.   bibliography

6. As she took notes from her sources, to help her
    avoid _____, Brown made oversized   plagiarism
    quotation marks around quoted material and then
    carefully summarized or paraphrased the rest,
    using her own words, phrasing and sentence patterns.

7. Brown drafted several versions of her _____   thesis
   statement in order to answer her research question.

8. After discovering that her first draft lacked clear
   organizational signals, Brown used _____   topic
   sentences to begin many of the paragraphs in her
   second draft.

9. After finding that her first draft depended too
   heavily on direct _____, Brown para-   quotations
   phrased and summarized many of them, using them
   only when their language was especially _____   apt
   ____.

10. Brown uses a specific example from a newspaper
    story as an opener in the in introductory para-
    graph of her paper and then a _____   quotation
    in her concluding paragraph.

11. Brown used a formal _____ outline to   sentence
    organize her paper, with each section corresponding
    to groups of paragraphs within the text of the paper.

12. Brown uses the new MLA system of _____   parenthetical
    citations of her sources within the body of the
    paper and a list of _____ Cited at the   Works
    end.

13. Within one set of parentheses identifying the
    sources of information for her paper, Brown includes
    the word Hidden (as well as a page number reference)
    to cite a book by Hall because she refers to _____   two
    _____ books by this same author on her Works Cited
    list.

14. Brown also included a _____ page at the   Notes
    end of her paper; these were not references but
    additional information or explanations of the
    points she made in the text of the paper.

34
WRITING
IN OTHER
DISCIPLINES

KEY TERMS AND CONCEPTS

primary sources
secondary sources
documentation
plagiarism
active voice
passive voice
humanities
discourse
informative writing
persuasive writing
literary analysis
plot
theme
structure
setting
point of view
style
imagery
tone
symbolism
rhythm/rhyme
interpretation
book report
reaction paper

research paper
note documentation system
social sciences
observation
interviewing
questionnaire
definition
analogy
analysis
case study
APA parenthetical citation
References list
natural/technological sciences
methods of inquiry
scientific method
empirical evidence
hypothesis
replicate
scientific report
abstract
review of the literature
scientific review

FILL-IN QUESTIONS

1. Writing in the _____ would present a   humanities
    personal yet general human response to an issue;
    writing in the social sciences would focus on

_____ behavior while writing in the
natural sciences would report _____
of natural phenomena. (34a)

group
observations

2. In the humanities, _____ sources are
usually documents such as literary or musical
manuscripts, but in the social and natural
sciences, these sources involve experiment and
_____ observation. (34a)

primary

direct

3. Although writers in the humanities often use the
active voice, writers in the social and natural
sciences often use the _____ voice
to emphasize the observation rather than the
observer. (34a)

passive

4. To write a literary analysis of a work, read it
carefully several times, looking for _____
in such aspects as plot, theme, structure, setting,
point of view, style, imagery, tone, symbolism,
rhythm and rhyme. (34b)

patterns

5. Literary interpretation seeks to explain what an
author has meant by a work while a _____
paper presents a reader's response to or thoughts
and feelings about the work or some aspect of it.
(34b)

reaction

6. Some instructors in the humanities may require the
notes system of _____ instead of the
MLA system of parenthetical references. (34b)

documentation

7. Writers in the social sciences often use direct
observations, interviewing and questionnaires to
to gather information, but they must be careful
not to influence the _____ by using
intrusive tools, by asking unclear or slanted
questions, or by generalizing from the responses
of a small number of people. (34c)

results

8. When they write to inform or persuade by classi-
fying, analyzing or explaining a human problem or
condition, social scientists must carefully
_____ vague or ambiguous terms. (34c)

define

9. An _____ can help make an unfamiliar
idea more clear by comparing it to an idea that is
more familiar. (34c)

analogy

10. Writing a report of a _____ study (an
intensive study of one individual or a group) often
involves a format that includes but separates the
following: a section containing basic information
about the individual or group, another about their

case

history or background, another containing actual observations of their behavior, and another containing _____ based on the observation.

conclusions

11. A research paper in the social sciences may ask you to report on _____ research (an experiment you have done perhaps) or you may be required to consult and write about _____ sources (articles and books that discuss the findings of primary research) and then document your writing using the APA method of _____ _____ citations within your text and a References list at the end. (34c)

primary

secondary

parenthetical

12. Following the scientific method, a scientist formulates and tests a _____, a tentative explanation for an observed phenomenon, in order to explain a cause and effect relationship systematically and objectively. (34d)

hypothesis

13. Scientists may reject or confirm their hypotheses by drawing conclusions from _____ evidence, the information gathered from their observation of natural and experimental events. (34d)

empirical

14. Because scientists expect to be able to _____ the research of others (to repeat step by step by step the experiment or process and get the same results), scientific writing requires _____ descriptions of procedures and findings as well as complete reporting of observations. (34d)

replicate

exact

15. While a scientific _____ describes observations and experiments (and may or may not include a discussion of the scientific literature on the topic), a scientific _____ discusses published information on a topic to give readers current knowledge about it; the documentation style may vary according to the specific field. (34d)

report

review

35
BUSINESS WRITING

KEY TERMS AND CONCEPTS

conventional (standard) format
resume
chronological order
memo (memorandum)

"to" line
distribution
"subject" line
message

FILL-IN QUESTIONS

1. As in all effective writing, business writing requires that writers understand their _____ _____ and purpose. (35)

audience

2. In addition, writers should put essential information first, should make their points clearly and directly, and should use a conventional _____ _____. (35)

format

3. Business letters that are likely to get results are short, simple, direct and _____. (35a)

human

4. When you want to write effective business letters, one expert recommends that you call the person by name, that you be positive and natural, and that you be _____. (35a)

honest

5. He also recommends that you tell what your letter is about in the _____ paragraph, that you be clear and specific, that you use accurate English, and that you _____ ruthlessly. (35a)

first

edit

6. A _____ is an easy-to-read, factual document that presents your qualifications for employment, including your skills, education and experience. (35c)

resume

7. Choose and arrange the headings of your resume in order to emphasize your _____ to your potential employer. (35c)

strengths

8. When listing your address on your resume, be sure it is a place where you can be reached by _____ _____. (35c)

letter

9. A _____ can call for action or document action; it can provide a written record of a _____, or it can make a brief, informal report.   (35d)

memo

conversation

10. At the "to" line of your memo, list the person or people who need to act on the information you are reporting, but list for _____ anyone else you think should be informed of the memo's contents. (35d)

distribution

11. The _____ line should define and limit the memo's contents as well as set the tone or signal your _____ toward the subject. (35d)

subject

attitude

12. The _____ should give the most important information or point first, with additional or secondary information following it in decreasing order of importance. (35d)

message

APPENDIX
WRITING COMPETENCY
ESSAY EXAMS

At some point on your college career, you may be required to take a writing competency exam--a timed test of your ability to organize and write an essay. The Florida CLAST exam, for example, requires a fifty minute essay.

Although you will not be asked to discuss or analyze specific course material, a competency exam is similar to any "in-class" essay in that you will need to organize your thoughts quickly, make a clear and definite point, and then support it in a coherent discussion that includes specific evidence, reasons, illustrations and examples.

Before you take the exam, try to find out how your topic will be set up. Some competency exams, perhaps one given as a final exam in a writing course, may require you to write on a specific topic such as "the automobile" or "stress." Others may give you more opportunity to demonstrate how well you can select and narrow a subject onto a suitable topic. For example, students writing the essay portion of the Florida CLAST exam are given a choice between two relatively open topics, which they must narrow, then shape into a thesis that they must support with material from their own knowledge and experience. In the two sample essays that follow in Part Four, students taking a writing competency exam in a freshman composition class were given a choice between these writing topics:

1) a natural feature that should be preserved
2) an idea that has had beneficial effects

Once you are given your topics and the exam begins, you must <u>plan</u> your essay. Since you are working against time, choose your topic as quickly as possible and narrow it into a working thesis. Next, before you begin to write, stop to think. Jot down on scratch paper as many specifics related to your topic as you can think of in two or three minutes. Writing experts suggest that this planning stage is <u>absolutely</u> <u>essential</u> in a short timed

148

essay since you will not have time to develop more than one draft. If you have only fifty minutes to write, use the first five to ten minutes to plan. Then write for thirty-five to forty minutes, saving the last five minutes to proofread your essay.

As you plan, think about how you want to organize your essay. Look at your list of specifics and select the three or four best ideas, examples, reasons, etc. Next, imagine how the completed essay will look. Visualize it developed into four to six paragraphs, as in the outlined format on page 154 . Then create a scratch outline that lays out your ideas according to the format. In the outline you may decide to save your most important or dramatic point for last.

Before you begin to write, check your thesis statement again to see if it needs refining and rewording. Remember that it should be an affirmative statement of the essay's main point, reflecting your informative or persuasive purpose, your focus, and may briefly state the major subdivisions of the essay.

PART TWO--WRITING THE ESSAY

Once you have clarified your thesis and visualized its development, begin to write the essay. Double space to leave room for later revisions; write as legibly as you can. In the introductory paragraph, try for an attention getter such as a quotation, a striking fact or an example, and then close the first paragraph with your thesis statement.

Next, in your body paragraphs, introduce each of your supporting points with a topic sentence that links it directly to your thesis, and then develop that point with specifics in subsequent sentences of the paragraph. Use smooth transitional phrases and sentences to move from one idea to the next, making sure to support each of your general comments with specifics. Remember what you have learned about your possible choices in paragraph development and using RENNS (reasons, examples, names, numbers and appeals to the five senses) to develop with specifics. For example, if you are urging the preservation of forests, mention a specific area by name and perhaps specific animals that live in its ecosystem, or the importance of the photosynthesis/oxygen cycle, or a specific effect of acid rain on that area.

Feel confident as you develop and support your ideas; you are turning the essay you have envisioned into reality. When you are making your points, listen to the sound of the sentences you are expressing. If you want to emphasize certain points, try using parallel structure. Or try subordination to show relationships between your ideas.

After you finish your body paragraphs, look back over your opening paragraph and those you have used to support it. Make sure you have not wandered away from your main point. Then add a conclusion that sums up the essence of your main point. You should echo your thesis, but if you simply restate it, your reader is likely to think that you have run out of words. Try an interesting quote, emphatic statement or call to action.

However, don't fuss too long over your finish. Instead, <u>use that last five minutes of your allotted time to proofread</u> your essay. Look for sentence errors such as comma splices, fragments or dangling modifiers. Look for verb and pronoun agreement and for punctuation, capitalization and spelling errors. Look for padding, for unnecessary repetition and for any words that are misleading, vague or otherwise unclear. Cross out all errors neatly and carefully write your new version above them. Add any other necessary information. You need not be afraid that your graders will "count off" for messiness if you do this; instead, they will probably be impressed that you can find and correct your own errors.

PART THREE--EVALUATING THE ESSAY

After you turn in your essay, it may be evaluated in one of two ways: (1) by the traditional "analytical" method, which evaluates such aspects as thought/content, organization, style, grammar, punctuation, usage and mechanics all separately, or (2) by the "holistic" method, which evaluates the total impression the essay makes on a quick reading. The Florida CLAST essay, for example, is scored holistically: two readers read the essay and score it according to the criteria that is listed below. The two scores (a possible "one," "two," "three" or "four") are added together, making the highest possible score an "eight."

Score of 4: Writer purposefully and effectively develops a thesis. Writer uses relevant details, including concrete examples, that clearly support generalizations. Paragraphs carefully follow an organizational plan and are fully developed and tightly controlled. A wide variety of sentence patterns occur, indicating that the writer has facility in the use of language, and diction is distinctive. Appropriate transitional words and phrases or other techniques make the essay coherent. Few errors in syntax, mechanics and usage occur.

Score of 3: Writer develops a thesis but may occasionally lose sight of purpose. Writer uses some relevant and specific details that adequately support generalizations. Paragraphs generally follow an organizational plan and are usually unified and developed. Sentences are often varied, and diction is usually appropriate. Some transitions are used, and parts are usually related to each other in an orderly manner. Syntactical, mechanical and usage errors may occur but usually do not affect clarity.

Score of 2: Writer may state a thesis, but the essay shows little, if any sense of purpose. Writer uses a limited number of details, but they often do not support generalizations. Paragraphs may relate to the thesis but often will be vague, underdeveloped, or both. Sentences lack variety and are often illogical, poorly constructed or both. Diction is pedestrian. Transitions are used infrequently,

150

mechanically, and erratically. Numerous errors may occur in syntax, mechanic, and usage, frequently distracting clarity.

Score of 1: Writer's thesis and organization are seldom apparent, but, if present, they are unclear, weak, or both. Writer uses generalizations for support, and details, when included, are usually ineffective. Underdeveloped, ineffective paragraphs do not support the thesis. Sentences are unusually illogical, poorly constructed or both. They usually consist of a series of subjects and verbs with an occasional complement. Diction is simplistic and frequently not idiomatic. Transitions and coherence devices, when discernible, are usually inappropriate. Syntactical, mechanical, and usage errors abound and impede communication.

PART FOUR--EXAMPLES OF ESSAYS WRITTEN BY STUDENTS

Following are two essays written by students who selected topic "An idea that has had beneficial effects: and narrowed it to the benefits of computers. Before you read the essays below, review the criteria for holistic scoring. You will notice that evaluators will look first for how well a writer has stated the thesis, next for how well it is supported with specifics and how well the paragraphs follow the plan set up in the thesis. The evaluator will gain a clear overall impression of how well the writer controls the whole process of writing the essay. Thesis, support and organization will tell part of the story, but so will sentence variety, word choice, use of transitions and other techniques to make the essay coherent. Finally, the evaluator will note the number and kind of sentence structure (syntax), usage, punctuation and mechanics errors. Before deciding on a specific score, the evaluator will try to classify the essay in terms of whether it is "upper level" (a possible score of three or four) or "lower level" (a possible score of one or two).

With these criteria in mind, read and try your hand at evaluating the following essays:

The Aid of Computers in a Busy World

by Student A

Many years ago, man could derive mathematical computations with only a stick and dirt. Then later perhaps he used an abacus, but any method was long and tedious. However, as man advanced, so did his mathematical instruments. Today computers find computations extremely quickly, accurately, and as a result, the design of the computer has had beneficial effects on business, manufacturing, creative and educational functions.

As a result of computers, business has become much easier to sustain. For example, any mathematical formulas needed to compute an employee's paycheck, taxes, or other computation can

151

easily be programmed into the computer for quick and accurate results. Also, a secretary can use a word processor on a computer to type business letters and forms without error. Perhaps the most important ability used in business is that of data storage. On a computer, names, addresses, files, and other information can be kept organized and be quickly accessed.

In addition to business, manufacturing has benefitted from the computer extensively. For instance, the design of certain parts can be accurate and efficient by using the CAD (Computer Aided Design) system. After the part is designed, computers can be programmed to create the actual part, by using robotic arms. Also, by using the computer, many aspects that will have certain effects on the product can be observed. For example, the wind against a moving car can be compensated for, the volume of a bellows can be determined, and other aspects can be viewed that affect the product being manufactured.

Although business and manufacturing use computers for various purposes, a computer's use does not end here; many other fields of study use computers. Writers may use the computer's word processing ability, manipulating words, sentences and paragraphs. Meteorologists use the computer to predict weather and atmospherical occurences. Musicians use the sound capabilities to listen to compositions. The music can even be printed out at a printer, as can a letter or document, for "hard copy" (one that can be viewed in "black and white").

In addition to fields of study, people can employ the computer's capabilities for education. Many games are available that can better eye and hand coordination, teach students letters, colors, or numbers, aid students in studying for tests, and many other processes.

Because business, manufacturing and the creative and educational fields have used the computer, this concept in these modern times has had many beneficial effects. The quicker and more accurate results show that the human race is far from the computor's ancestor, the abacus.

Computers

by Student B

Computers today are being used more and more each day. They are used in our daily lifes. Computers are minds that think and that give us beneficial effects.

Computers have boosted the economy by producing more jobs in the industry field. People can get jobs such as programming a computer, keeping charge of records for large corporations. People who know how to use a computer can also get jobs on marketing and advertising for major corporations. They can keep track of budgeting and the frequency of the profits vs. losses of the company.

A computer works like an ordered file. They can store anything from dates to figures that run in the millions. Computers are used all around the world, especially in major corporations like AT&T. They use them to keep track of records.

Computers are a demanding item today. You have a vast choice, when it comes to choosing a computer. You could get an Apple or IBM, which is fine for a small business, because they are not so technical, or you could get an Xerox, which is very commonly used in the industrial business today.

Learning to use a computer is not as difficult as it appears to be. Once you know the language, you then know how to work and set programs. Once you know the computer, you can use it to put important dates, make charts for budgeting, store personal information, place names and payrolls of your employees, etc.

Today computers play any important part of our life. They keep everything intact. Eventually everyone will be using computors.

PART FIVE--DISCUSSION OF STUDENT ESSAYS

Perhaps after a quick but careful reading of the two preceding essays, you decided that the essay written by Student A was "upper level." You may have noticed how the plan of the well-stated thesis was developed in body paragraphs containing appropriate topic sentences, specifics and concrete examples. Transitions, a variety of sentence patterns and active verbs help to demonstrate control of the writing process. The title, introduction and conclusion are inviting and add to the unified sense of the whole essay.

In contrast, the essay by Student B probably struck you as much weaker than that of Student A. The introduction does not arouse much interest and the thesis is too vague to help direct the development of the rest of the essay. Although the body paragraphs do contain some examples, the topic sentences of most of them do not function to unify the contents of each paragraph and direct the reader to its main point or to tie it to the main point of the whole essay. Repetitions, generalized word choice, lack of transitions and other coherence techniques as well as lack of much variety in sentence structure and some errors (particularly with pronoun use) may have led you to classify the essay by Student B as "lower level."

PART SIX--GAINING EXPERIENCE THROUGH PRACTICE

After reading the preceding suggestions and examples, you may want to gain experience with timed writing competency tests in order to build your confidence. You can practice by choosing one of the topics listed below. Prepare yourself by finding a spot that will be free of distractions, wear a watch or carry a clock so you can time yourself. Bring plenty of paper and several pens and pencils. You may not be allowed to use a dictionary during your real test, so try going without it during your practice. Review the format outline on page 154 . Then choose one of the following topics and begin:

1)   a policy or practice that should be changed
2)   an individual who has influenced modern life

Original Title

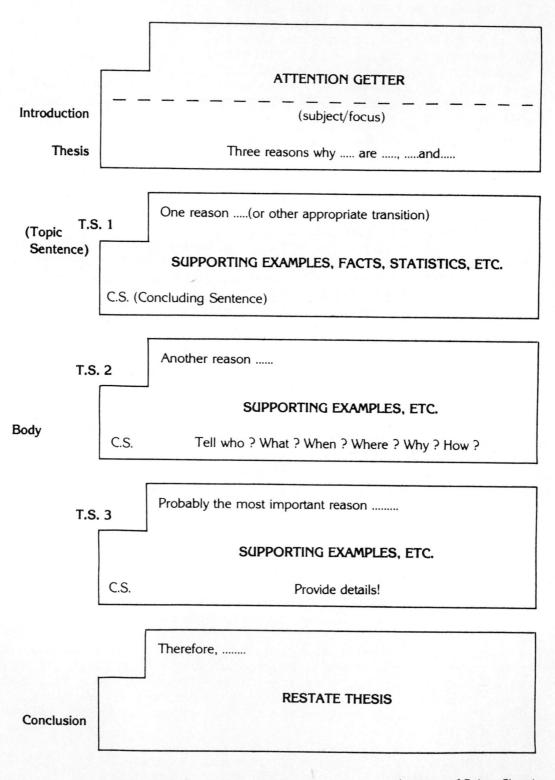

Introduction

ATTENTION GETTER

— —

(subject/focus)

Thesis

Three reasons why ..... are ....., ...and.....

(Topic Sentence) T.S. 1

One reason .....(or other appropriate transition)

SUPPORTING EXAMPLES, FACTS, STATISTICS, ETC.

C.S. (Concluding Sentence)

T.S. 2

Another reason ......

SUPPORTING EXAMPLES, ETC.

Body

C.S.   Tell who ? What ? When ? Where ? Why ? How ?

T.S. 3

Probably the most important reason ....

SUPPORTING EXAMPLES, ETC.

C.S.   Provide details!

Therefore, ...

RESTATE THESIS

Conclusion

(courtesy of Robert Sharp)

The Writing Process

For the 50 minute essay: (CLAST)

Pre-Writing (5 minutes)	Writing (40 minutes)	Re-Writing (5 minutes)
1. Develop a Thesis· (your original response to the assigned topic· choose one quickly.) 2. Make a list of specifics· (select your three best ideas, one for each paragraph in the Body of the essay.)	Organize your ideas rhetorically· 1. Introductory Paragraph · Attention Getter/Thesis 2. Body · · Three supporting examples· be specific, use transitions 3. Concluding paragraph.	Put an original title on the essay. Read papers over, from beginning to end, correcting careless errors as you go. Remember to double space and use ink. Cross out errors neatly. ~~neetly.~~